Make Me a Mother

ALSO BY SUSANNE ANTONETTA

A Mind Apart:
Travels in a Neurodiverse World

Body Toxic:
An Environmental Memoir

MAKE ME A MOTHER

A Memoir

Susanne Antonetta

W. W. NORTON & COMPANY

New York · London

A few segments of this book first appeared, in whole or in part,
in the following publications, with the title as given below:

Fourth Genre: "Dark Matter"
Image: "Hosts"
Orion: "As Flies," "Improbable Gifts"
Seneca Review: "Nine Lives"
The New Republic: "No Words Lecture Hall" (poem)
The New York Times: "Who Is This Child, What Will He Be Next?"

"Hosts" also appeared in the *Pushcart Prize XXVI:*
Best of the Small Presses (2012)

The author is grateful for their interest in her work.

For information about permission to reproduce selections from this book,
write to Permissions, W. W. Norton & Company, Inc.,
500 Fifth Avenue, New York, NY 10110

For information about special discounts for bulk purchases, please contact
W. W. Norton Special Sales at specialsales@
wwnorton.com or 800-233-4830

Manufacturing by Courier Westford
Book design by Ellen Cipriano Design
Production manager: Julia Druskin

ISBN: 978-0-393-06817-7

W. W. Norton & Company, Inc.
500 Fifth Avenue, New York, N.Y. 10110
www.wwnorton.com

W. W. Norton & Company Ltd.
Castle House, 75/76 Wells Street, London W1T 3QT

1 2 3 4 5 6 7 8 9 0

FOR JIN

Saranghayo
con tutto cuore mio

Or more simply:
so you'll know

NO WORDS LECTURE HALL

You're not the boss of me my son screams.
He's tired, and thirteen, and skidding into
my and his sudden strangeness.
(Who is this woman who puts her wine on the bench,
crams wisteria in a drinking glass, can't find a vase?
Who asks him to quit the 80 decibel belching.
She has grown foreign, and ridiculous.)

He says to me, *you embarrass me* and he says *I don't*
    want you in my room
I want to say, I love you. *You're*

embarrassing me I love you and I'd
never lock you up. Never let anybody shock you
with 130 volts of electricity through your head.
Stick the bit in your mouth, spread
conducting gel on either side of your fine high
forehead.

Don't you understand how huge that is?
Don't you see how that makes me a good mother?
I do say these things, in my mind.
Even there with a pleading, with a pitched
hum.

Contents

9

Part V: My Adoptive Family

Make Me a Mother

Prologue: Adoption
as a Way of Saying Life

T HESE DAYS, WHEN I wake up, I don't know where I am. There are constants: first that streaky darkness of early morning, the noise of robins or doves, trilling or cooing. The gradually paling air of early morning, which wherever I am feels the same: the odor of earth in its cool newness, air exhaled up from the soil of wherever I happen to be, not like the more celestial air of later in the day. I ask myself, in my groggy reckoning of where I might be finding myself, if my husband is in the bed with me, the first clue. He's always turned on his side away from me by this point in the morning though I catch his odor, a smell both distinctly male and distinctly him. And the second clue: a warm lump at my feet that's my little dog Meeko hunched under the covers. I ask myself whether my son lies upstairs, asleep. If I'm in my own bed the window will be cracked open a little and in September, as it is now, the scent of honeysuckle will be heavy on the air, deeply sweet, in a way no bottled perfume can be. At home in Bellingham, Washington, just off the Puget Sound,

13

there will also be an odor of brine, almost an afterthought of it, that pungency that's at once so reminiscent of tears, and sex, and blood.

Or it may be that I sleep in a double bed that urges my body into its lumpy center and rattles if I move, in an attic room, in my parents' house in New Jersey. I visit them every three months or so, and stay anywhere from four to ten or more days, and when I wake up in the morning I need to rule out their house in order to place myself at my own home. It is possible for my husband to be there too, in New Jersey, with the tilt of the mattress sliding us both into its center, my son sleeping downstairs on the floor. Generally, though, if I'm there I'm alone; my clue as I wake up is the sound of my father moving things around in the kitchen— he gets up early and rearranges plates and cups, no matter how carefully I've tried to put them in the right place. And then the heat: even in winter, my parents, aged eighty-six and ninety-two, keep their house hot, and still my mother calls out all day for more sweaters.

There are outlier places I could be: in the last months I've traveled to Santa Fe and Syracuse and Hong Kong for work. I've spent the night, family along, with my friend Marcie in Seattle. But most often as I wake up and shake off the shadows of the long and involved dream my mind spins every morning just before rousing itself, I'm in Washington or I'm in New Jersey. Neither place is far from one of two oceans, and in both places from my window I can hear the *awk awk* of gulls.

At home in Washington I have my fifteen-year-old adopted son, a child born in South Korea who has spent his life, all but

the first four months of it, here, living in this house, knowing only me as mother. When my son Jin wakes up, I'll make
him something to eat. In New Jersey, in a house where I never
lived—my parents moved there after I went away to college—I
have my parents. If I'm there when they wake up, I'll also make
them something to eat. Then I'll do things for my mother I no
longer have to do for my son: help her use the bathroom and
help her dress. Guide her as she walks, with the help of a walker
she pushes, because if I don't, she'll fall.

Wherever I find myself upon waking, I think instantly of
the other place. My parents have had many bone breaks in the
last few years and struggle, with more and less success, to stay
in their home. They are old, and I don't know how long they'll
live. If I'm at their house and I wake up, uncomfortable and
sticky from the heat there, my longing for my husband and son
is physical, visceral. I want to talk to them, and more—I want
to touch their hair and their arms. When I'm awake enough to
know they're three thousand miles away, I have to swallow my
fear and anxiety: what if they go out to a movie together and get
in an accident? What if one of them leaves the gas on at night?
What if they decide they're having more fun without me?

I have adopted my parents as well as my son. I call the relationship my parents and I have one of adoption, because we have
a bond that I have accepted with intention. It's a bond that no
one, least of all the three of us, could have foreseen. When I was
my son's age, I would never have imagined I'd help my parents
through the last years of their lives, and my parents would have
imagined it even less. I was a lost child.

⌒——

In the traditional social understanding of the term, about 4 percent of all parents in America adopt—meaning, two biologically
unrelated people become the legal parents of a child who comes
to them either from the foster care system, through private adoption (perhaps an open adoption in which the child will continue
contact with one or both biological parents), or international
adoption. Many people—even those who write books about
adoption—often suppose that adoption is a choice made due
to infertility. In fact, just as the majority of adopted children in
our country do not have living or capable biological parents—a
fact that the news coverage of adoption, with its emphasis on
reunions, obscures—most infertile couples do not go on to adopt.
They opt out of having children. The number of infertile couples
who do adopt lies somewhere between 11 and 25 percent—a low
figure, which indicates that infertility is just one of many factors
that lead to the choice to adopt.[1]

Legal adoption in our country takes place all the time in
contexts other than those suggested by the traditional construction of the term: stepparents adopt their stepchildren; couples
conceive with donor eggs fertilized by only the male partner's
sperm; grandparents and aunts and uncles adopt the children
of relatives, often impaired relatives (family member adoption
rates have spiraled to about a quarter of all adoptions in the
crack and meth epidemics of the last decades);[2] and, in zygote
adoption, couples even implant the fertilized zygote of another

couple, often produced by fertility treatment—a form of adoption that has received considerable funding from the federal government.[3] Gay male adoptive parents, and many single parents, go to adoption as the best option they have (and of course, at least one member of a lesbian couple will not be biologically related to their baby, however it comes).

Private adoption records are held in individual courthouses, though even if you could go from courthouse to courthouse reading records, adoption solely by choice, or preferential adoption, would remain difficult to gauge. During the late 1990s, a high point for adoption in the US, about 80 percent of parents in private adoptions had some experience of infertility, according to the Evan B. Donaldson Institute, while half of those who adopted from foster care did.[4] One-fifth of private adopters had not experienced infertility at all. According to the last National Survey of Family Growth, conducted by the CDC/NCHS in 2002, the majority of men who adopt have fathered a biological child, while half of women who adopt have given birth themselves. Many parents are drawn to adoption as their preference for forming or adding to a family. Some parents have biological children and then adopt, perhaps when young adult children have left or are about to leave the home. Sometimes couples, feeling that having more than two children would be irresponsible given the size of the world's population, add a third or fourth by adoption. These parents want more children without feeling the drive to bear them. Sometimes parents feel motivated to adopt out of concern for the number of children who need homes. Health questions, such as the possibility of passing along certain genetic traits, can be a part of preferential adoption.

I came to adoption through a mix of routes: my husband and I suffered a miscarriage, but I had always dreamed, since childhood, of adopting someday. I love the idea of children, however they arrive, and in spite of Richard Dawkins and his theory of the selfish gene that exists just to reproduce itself through the vehicles of our bodies, I have never personally felt the need to reproduce my own. I have bipolar disorder, as most likely did my husband's father, though my bent toward adoption goes beyond that, and beyond my planetary concerns. Perhaps, as someone who works several times a year in Hong Kong, and who has worked in places from Italy to Slovenia, I found it natural that my own household and my family would resemble the rich and far-flung world I choose to live in. The questions this choice would raise—how my child would feel about being moved into my world—lay ahead of me.

It is very common to hear from those who adopt by choice that they put adoption into their parenting plans early in life, as I did. Karen, who lives and works in Houston, recalls deciding to adopt when she was a child.

"When I was about five, my mom's sister adopted her daughter, then twin boys. I remember my mom telling me in some early 1970s way—in my mind, they walked into a large nursery and picked their kid. I thought it was the coolest thing I ever heard that they chose their baby. I always thought if I became a parent I would adopt at least one."

Psychiatrist E. James Lieberman writes: "In talking with

prospective parents, I suggest—provocatively—that couples are ready for parenthood only when they can imagine adopting. Indeed, we all have to adopt our children psychologically."[5]

Indeed we do. And we may need to adopt our parents in return—as, with expanded life expectancies, they need an intensity of care that previous generations did not face. Many of us, as I have, find ourselves returning the nurture our parents gave to us as children. Not all of us received the parenting we are called upon to give back, in which case this kind of parental adoption becomes particularly meaningful, particularly bittersweet.

In fact, we psychologically adopt everyone we invite to enter our lives. My cousin's husband used to speak of adopting people. "Oh, your aunt Kathleen, I've adopted her," he would say, using the term to mean a complete and thorough commitment to someone. In the largest sense of the term *adoption* the choice to take someone or something on—we adopt throughout our lives. We take genetically unrelated strangers and make them life partners, and their family becomes our family. We bring friends and neighbors into our lives and make them family too. We have biological children, perhaps, who look nothing like us or our partners, or who look exactly like a partner we'd rather forget, children who might seem like creatures dropped into our lives from an alien planet, so different are they, and learn to love and accept them for who they are.

In our present era, when people move from place to place and frequently divorce and remarry, adoption is more than a fraction of our national family formation; it is a reflection of the way we live our lives. In the past, bands, tribal groups, and geography tended to define our social relationships for us. In restless modern America, we tend to define them for ourselves. Never has the concept *family* meant *genetics* less than it does now—so many of us, in our transient culture, define family as friends, as colleagues and neighbors.

We humans did not invent this way of forming relationships. Hundreds of species of birds, mammals, and other animals adopt, taking on the young—even the eggs—of other members of their own species, particularly if those young are orphaned or neglected.[6] Many species will also adopt cross-species; Chinese zoos, for instance, use dogs to nurse the infants of tigers, who are notoriously unwilling to raise young born in captivity.

Throughout much of the world, including the Asia–Pacific islands and much of Africa, kinship fostering—sending children to live within a loose network of friends and extended family, depending on the children's needs and the adults' preferences, without formal legal transference—is practiced in most families. Many ethnic groups in the United States also practice kinship fostering. Adoption, too, is practiced in many cultures with little worry about biological implications, and it has existed for as long as we have historical records.

The making of family, any kind of family, involves a process of choice. The word *adoption* has been trivialized, used to mean everything from which books teachers select for their students to the catching on of fads. But I feel sure, as I pass the midpoint of my life, that I have never done anything more profound, both in becoming a mother to my son, and in adopting my own parents.

When I started this book, my son said, "Are you writing this for me? So I'll know how you feel about me? When I'm older?" His cool, clear insight threw me a little.

"Well, yeah," I told him, and wanted to add, so everyone else will too, though I'm not yet ready to talk about these qualifications: So no one will think I fantasized about a birth child. So no one will think my baby was some kind of second choice. So no one will think it matters that I didn't hold him seconds after he pushed into the world.

Part I

ARRIVAL

1.

Infancy: Finding Family at the S Gate

M Y BABY ARRIVED at SeaTac Airport on November 21, 1997. That's how we came to bring him home. Adoption generally involves travel to where the child began his or her life, but we lacked that change of scene to prepare us. My husband, Bruce, and I simply drove to a place we'd been to a hundred times—or actually, were driven, by our friends Marc and Dawn, who worried that in our nervousness we would be a menace on the road—staying at a motel where we'd slept a dozen times. It was a scabby Motel 6, where once the receptionist gave our room keys to another couple, who burst in on us in our sleep.

There were no intruders during this stay at the Motel 6. No sleep. We lay awake in bed all night with our fingers lightly locked.

That evening, I'd sat in a restaurant with Bruce and a group of friends, including Marc and Dawn, drinking ginger martinis. I loved just then that part of adoption. Jin's arrival in my life had no implications for my body; at that moment he sat propped on his pillow, strapped into his airplane seat. I could drink martinis.

"I wonder where he is right now," we said. We debated: in Tokyo (the poor kid did not even have a direct flight), over the Sea of Japan. Perhaps even thirty thousand feet above our Pacific.

"You could be in labor," a friend said. Which was true: I could have been trying to squeeze something the size of a football out of an opening in myself not anywhere near that big, and instead I sat in an Asian fusion place, much trendier than places I usually go, drinking ginger martinis. No amount of martini could soften those nerves, mine and Bruce's; on the ride to SeaTac Airport, we stared at the empty car seat in a kind of trance.

We had received only three days' notice of Jin's arrival. We had been ready, in a physical sense, since late summer: the nursery was put together, we had the furniture we needed, boxes of diapers. We had been told Jin would arrive in late September. The first week after his projected arrival we were on tenterhooks, jumping at every ring of the phone. The next week we felt expectant still but slightly less so, and by November waiting had taken on its own intractable permanence. In September nothing had seemed less probable than Jin not arriving; by late November, nothing seemed less probable than that he would.

I had passed those months in a state of unimaginable frustration: every baby I saw reminded me of my son's life passing without me. I begged Bill, our social worker, to let me fly to South

Korea and take custody there. No, he said, my going would just slow things down even further. I watched more television than I ever had before. I rewashed baby laundry and ate kimchi and slathered my food with soy sauce and sesame oil, as did Bruce, on the advice that it would make our odor familiar to our new baby. Of course, like adoptive parents around the world, we had been checked, rechecked, fingerprinted, and sent in for medical exams. We had demonstrated the kind of expertise you absorb from zombie-staring at every page of *What to Expect the First Year*.

But we were also filled with anxiety. What if none of it worked? What if the books' magical comfort techniques never put our baby to sleep? What if he never burped? Never ate?

Now that my dream of adopting was coming true, the reality of that baby to be handed off to me became a fact loaded and full of questions. Preexisting me, he came with his own history, his sense of the landscapes of his life, the people who populated the days he had, in his wordless, sensory way, already lived.

What if he just doesn't like me? I wondered. What if I somehow couldn't love him? Does that ever happen? I imagined the child you delivered from your own body barely realizing the umbilical cord had been cut, feeling he was you, and the bond of that shared body. Instead my child had a world that had been given to him at birth, and I was not in it; rather, I had come along as he turned five months old.

I loved the idea of adoption, but as the moment came for my baby to arrive it felt as if a physical force had yanked us past some natural transition period, a period I saw in pregnant women as those weeks when they start saying, in one form or another,

"Get this baby out of me!" Their baby is never *not there*, even when it's barely more than an idea, a collection of cells. When you realize your own baby is actually going to go from being *not there* to *there* as fast as a jumbo jet can land, and that baby already has clothes and a diaper on, and quite a bit of scary green stuff in the diaper for that matter, it's kind of terrifying.

I have heard friends with birth children describe similar feelings: fear they wouldn't love their babies or be loved, even an inability to love their children right away, due to postpartum depression or a difficult birth or just something indefinable. I remember an aunt of mine describing to me, when I was a teenager, the birth of one of her daughters. The other two, she said, she loved right away.

"This one, though," she said, "came out this little, red, wrinkled thing. I looked at her thinking, 'Hmmmm, I don't know about you.'" The child felt apart from her in a way her other two babies hadn't; felt alien. I forget how long she told me it took to love her.

❧

The morning after our sleepless night at the Motel 6, Bruce and I ran on gin fumes and adrenaline to the gate. I raced through the security checkpoint, clutching my stuff instead of turning it over to the guards, including my huge and suspiciously unused diaper bag. Guards chased me down but smirked when my friends explained the circumstances (it was 1997, a more innocent time for airports). We clocked down the moving sidewalks and through the trams and up the escalators to board the vessel *Parenthood*, which would be arriving at a satellite gate. A social worker named Carol, a woman with a frosted bob and many envelopes full of papers to sign, met us there.

The plane that held our baby taxied right up to the glass. I was overwhelmed at the arrival of my baby but also at the strange vision of the pilot in the cockpit, just outside the glass, jumping out of the predawn darkness. Suddenly, he honked. Several times. And waved right at us. Who knew planes even had horns, like cars? Another bit of strange in our new, surreal life.

"He's honking at you," Carol said. "The pilots know who you are."

Since even at six in the morning people sit around in airports, I expect pilots recognized us new parents by the way we hung against the glass, looking as stuck as barnacles.

At 6:30, out of customs, came Jin himself, the wad of hair, high Korean forehead, and leaf-shaped eyes. Another family waited with us, a couple from Yakima, Washington, who already had a Korean-born son. The babies arrived in the arms of escorts, and, since they had grown a lot after the newborn photos were taken, they wore color-coded outfits: a bright pink onesie for the girl, blue for our boy.

"Which is Jin? That one?" Bruce jumped, pointing at the child in pink. I was not doing much better. When the babies came out into our part of the airport, I went completely numb. I had imagined what it would be like to run up and snatch, squish that baby. Instead my feet were leaded to the ground.

Someone had to push me to Jin like you'd push a young

teenager at a dance. I knew him and didn't know him. Jin had grown into a large baby, dressed in blue velour flocked with spit from the long ride, in a Snugli so tight we practically needed the jaws of life to get it off. At his first checkup we would find he was in the ninety-eighth percentile of the growth chart for American babies, for length and weight—beyond unusual for an infant from Asia. His eyes, with their beautiful epicanthic fold, surveyed our faces and his mouth drew back and revealed his amazing dimples, a wink in each cheek.

Jin watched us, mystified: he had not had the luxury even of an agency photo to prepare him, as we had. I clutched him so tightly Bruce had to pry him away.

We dressed him in some loose clothes, the kind you buy at music festivals here in the Northwest: reversible cotton pants with a wild pattern, hand-sewn by some hippie mother in Seattle. He was newly made as an American baby.

⌒

Within hours of meeting me, Jin began to suck my hair, the one part of me he loved immediately and without complication. Instant intimate, tiny stranger, Jin sat up with us in our double bed, still on Korean time, watching *Saturday Night Live*. When we laughed, he looked at us quizzically. I leaned my cheek above him, so I could smell him. I fell in love with his legs, their fat crooks. He still had that wonderfully mystical air, looking at everything as surprising, worthy of his gaze, but never too unexpected. We were all thumbs, spending twenty minutes on each diaper change and still leaving one tab drooping. I pinched fingers almost as small as matchsticks in baby nail clippers.

We talked every day for weeks about how much more we loved him. We had loved him before, loved the small photo of him we had: a scuff of hair, flexing feet, a leap of faith. Now Jin was real, bodily: a stomach to press your face into and kiss, the things we learned to do that made him happy, his comically loud laugh, his smell I cannot describe. It's just him, the way life is just life.

It took us several weeks to say "my son" casually, without feeling the need to explain.

We almost never put Jin down, except to sleep, and we co-slept a lot. I took hard-won maternity leave (on paper, my institution grants it only to pregnant women). Wherever we had started from, our bodies became necessary to each other. When Jin cried at night, we walked him through the house, dark and ghostly in those hours of the morning I had mostly known in my distant adolescent past, through drugs and alcohol and dissolution. That past flashed back to me—those young, gone hours—as I walked the house in a darkness that had nearly always been tied to one thing: those lost years and their mote-flushed pitch and flickering color, the stereo blasting something from the Jefferson Airplane or the Doors, my brain operating in some realm beside itself. I remembered in my gut that feeling, my consciousness stretched and pulled and distorted, the world gone taffy-strange.

I tried to picture my mother walking the house pregnant with the few pounds that was me, wondering what she felt. Bearing, as Coleridge once wrote of the daughter who became the support of his age, "the sex of the child" as well as she could. Wondering why she had agreed to have a second infant. Or maybe at times her ability to calm me won her over, as it soothed me to be able to comfort my own new baby.

Now the time of losing my own body, my consciousness, the time of the early hours of the morning, was reinvented as baby time.

We circled through our small rooms, cupping our baby; in the tub, we drizzled his back with water. I had my leave, and Bruce worked half-time then so we had time to be with him. We breathed the same air and consumed the same molecules and my epithelial cells pressed off on his hands, his face, the spot under his arms where I lifted him. We became kin.

⌒

First, though, we had to get acquainted. We mispronounced my son's name, the name my husband and I had faithfully preserved from his birth in Korea. He had been named at the orphanage where he began his life. I pronounced the baby's name "Jin Woo," short "i," with the "w" sounded, though it's correctly said as "Jeen-oo," a pronunciation I would not learn for half a dozen years.

I would have said I loved him that day at the airport, and I did, but some emphasis I can now put into those words did not yet exist: I loved him; I did not yet love *him*. Even before his arrival, this baby had taken over my life; my old and small house had sprouted so much baby furniture in the way of bouncers and playpens and blue plastic phones that I started calling the look "late Victorian/early Fisher-Price." Things into which this baby could be placed or strapped, or that he could be set on or in front of, spilled into the hallways and had become so familiar I kicked them out of my way, but the baby himself remained stubbornly mysterious. Oddly enough for a woman walking through a dark house in the middle of the night with a baby on her shoulder, I racked my brain for things to say, with the same buzz of awkwardness you might have at a dinner party where you barely know the other guests.

Of course I knew the baby didn't understand me. But I wasn't even sure what tone of voice he liked, if he liked me talking at all, or if singing might be better. Possibly my off-key voice might just be annoying. When you and a wailing, barely five-month-old infant have just been introduced, and he within a few hours begins to cry nonstop—and the thought uppermost in your mind is, *Oh my God, he's really not going anywhere else, is he? What am I supposed to do?*—you try everything and assume that whatever it is you're doing, it must be wrong.

Within a few days of our meeting, he'd spat up, puked, and peed on me, a baptism into intimacy forged through bodily fluids. The peeing on me, which occurred during a fumbling diaper change, struck the infant as wildly funny. I was amused—and heartened, on behalf of the whole human race—to know that babies could be so entertained, so in love with what their bodies could do.

And the baby? He had moved across five thousand miles and many bodies of water to wail in the night, his head resting improbably on the shoulder of someone not just far from his country of birth but someone who had managed to survive her own early years intact in defiance of the gods of probability, someone for whom motherhood had been largely a teasing and improbable question. Someone who had little experience of what it meant to be a mother.

〜

The baby becomes your obsession, your recreation, your hobby, your entertainment, your tether. It becomes as impossible to imagine simply leaving the house without thinking about it first—trailing each time a blanket, a bottle, a baby, maybe the portable playpen, maybe a handful of Cheerios, just to get a few weeds pulled—as it becomes impossible not to wish at times that you could: to wish that your movement could once again involve only yourself. What a heady freedom it was, that you did not appreciate: only caring for one body in the world.

It is delightfully unexpected that this baby will be so fascinating, the minutiae of him. He holds your eyes while he drinks his bottle and seeks them out again when he fills his diaper, studying your face, as if he wonders how you can always tell he's done this bit of involved and concentrated labor. He studies you as carefully when he poops as when he tries out his handful of vowels and consonants, finding, reasonably, that it's as sure a means of contact.

After a few weeks of our November windstorms, the year of Jin's arrival became an El Niño year, a weather pattern named by the Spanish for "little boy." El Niños bring ocean currents up from the equator and make the weather mild and warm in winter. We walked Jin for miles in his collapsible stroller, big dog and little dog in tow.

Jin hit physical milestones very fast, one after another, after he came to us, possibly because in Korea babies spend a great deal of time swaddled on their caretaker's back—not in a Snugli or anything reflecting Yankee ingenuity, but just a well-tied piece of cloth.

When Jin first came we could put him on a baby blanket on the floor and know he would stay there, throwing his feet up into the air, watching his toes while we watched him. By Christmas, a month after his arrival, I put Jin in the middle of the living room floor and, before I could stop him, he rolled over and over, rolling to the newly decorated Christmas tree in the corner and grabbing at ornaments. A few weeks later, he crawled.

My mama hormones crossed wires with some loose Martha Stewart hormones that holiday season. I imagined that on some visual level even a baby could be stunned by good Christmas décor. I hung the tree with dozens of hand-baked, hand-painted (with decorator icing) sugar cookies. Inner Martha had forgotten that we had a golden retriever and a springer spaniel, who stood grazing at the Christmas tree like deer munching foliage in the woods—just as the baby, every time we shifted our eyes away, careened wildly to the tree again, grabbing tin icicles and bulbs.

I bought a Santa Claus baby outfit for Jin. It had a hat he would not keep on and a black belt made of cloth. My parents and brother flew out for Christmas, rented a car together in

Seattle, and drove up to meet the newest member of the family, who greeted them in my arms from the door when they pulled up. My father came up the stairs wiping at his eyes. Even my mother was impressed.

"He's very good-looking," she told me. "Keep an eye on that kid. Somebody's going to steal him."

My brother Chris instantly became *that* uncle—the one who throws baby in the air till it seems like he's going to begin orbiting earth, which baby likes very much though his parents get a little nervous. Jin wore his Santa outfit on Christmas morning and tore at presents, as well as he could, and preferred of course the baby-sized habitat of the boxes and the bright stuttered images of the paper.

We fumbled through those days, feeling so much love for a baby whose relationship to us we could not capture in a few simple words. We had no ultrasounds to point to, or even a legal tie until well into our lives together. When did he become our son? When we accepted the referral, though he lived in his foster mother's house then, and grew and changed without us? When he arrived? After six months, when our adoption was declared official by a court? At what point did we all form a family?

I cooked Jin risotto, tofu, pureed vegetables seasoned with sesame oil, soy, and, later, garlic. We wanted him to love Korean food. Above all, we wanted to tie ourselves to his strong and growing body. I still love cooking for my son, and for my husband.

I raise, in our mild climate, many of our fruits and vegetables. I poked seeds into the ground that became the foods my baby ate and grew large on, mashed broccoli or carrots or raspberries that he'd put, as a toddler, on the ends of his fingers so he could bite them off.

The people of Oceania, including Hawaii, adopt children and give them to others to raise almost as commonly as they bear them, and they lack a Western attachment to purely genetic ties ("we don't think it's all that important, who your mother is," says my friend Tiana, a native Hawaiian). In these places, people believe your biological ties with your family grow from the ground you labor on, the ground that feeds you, the hands that prepare your food and work so that you might have your substance. With taken-in-to-the-family children, called in Hawaii *hanai*, there are many feeding rituals. *Hanai* children traditionally were fed by hand more often than biological children, even given the honor of having pre-masticated food placed in their mouths: drawing them into the family unit cell by cell.

Lacking feeding rituals or a community to witness us building a life together in those first days, we brought our baby home, spooned yogurt into his mouth, warmed bottle after bottle. We dreamed of planting raspberries and tiny tomatoes, feeling Jin grow into us, ounce by ounce.

2.

Infancy: Like Being Alive Twice

J IN'S LAUGH REMADE the world for me. I don't mean remade it in some wash of sticky sentiment; I mean he laughed often and unexpectedly, and I felt as if no one had clued me in before that so much of life was surprising and laced with humor. I was forty. The world had come to seem a bit predictable, with its chronic veil of Northwest rain: same job, same house, the body getting its fortyish aches and lines.

It took a mute little being to reintroduce the world to me. Jin put his toes into his mouth and laughed at them—who would have guessed we'd be graced with five random wiggly things at the end of our stalks! I played with him by lifting my own feet, yanking my lanky toes with my fingers, kicking air. Jin left crumbs on his face and the dogs licked the corners of his mouth after meals and he screeched with joy. When he could pull himself up, the golden retriever Burley galloped at him and knocked him down and he lay there laughing, limbs flapping in all directions, like an upended turtle. We took him to the Jersey shore and let Jin put on his water wings and hold Burley's leash in the calm of Barnegat Bay; the dog, who loved to swim, rippled him through the water.

"It's like a Nantucket sleigh ride," I told Jin, as he crested through the waves as whalers once had with a whale at the end of their harpoon, and he giggled. Yes, it's some world all right: with such things as dogs, and water, and movement.

Once, when Jin was six months old, we drove down to Seattle to see a special exhibition of Robert Mapplethorpe's photographs. I wore Jin on my back in his hand-me-down blue baby pack. As I looked at a Mapplethorpe photo of a young woman wearing a huge strap-on dildo, Jin exploded into hysterics. He laughed so hard people turned to stare, and we blushed and beat it out of the gallery. It hadn't seemed like a bad idea, taking an innocent little baby to see sexually explicit photos—what would he know about young women and strap-ons?—but clearly Jin in his baby pack had some opinion about Mapplethorpe's work. We drove home, where I idly turned the pages in one of our many baby books, which identified six months old as the age where "an ability to perceive incongruity" sets in. Oh, we thought: a woman with a penis, I guess that qualifies.

My baby would often giggle wildly at nothing, or what we perceived to be nothing, though if we watched him carefully we could often grasp what he was laughing at: one of the cat's whiskers, or the picture of a queen on a playing card, or an ant. I began to feel as if, in my forty years of life on this planet, I had forgotten the comic premise to which a cat's whiskers could serve as punch line.

It was like being alive twice, seeing the world twice, and the new vision came through the eyes of a smart, curious, unstoppable being who had never seen it before. We had our own little mindfulness coach, reminding us that, when all else fails us in this life, we can love our own toes, or the velvet coolness of a dog's ear, or his downy fur. People told us how we would fall in love with our baby, but not how, through him, we would fall in love with everything else again too.

When Jin's arrival was announced, I think some small part of me remained skeptical. He would catch a cold; flights would be canceled; some new, interminable visa delay would crop up. We'd planned to throw, three days after the date that did indeed turn out to be Jin's arrival date, a large and rather complicated party to celebrate a close friend's fortieth birthday. She wanted a 1950s-themed party, with women in cocktail dresses and men in suits, and food and drink of the period. When the fax came telling us that Jin would be in Seattle on the 21st, we debated for a while, then decided to go ahead and throw the party with our new baby here.

"He'll be on Korean time. He won't want to go to sleep, anyway," I said, citing our social worker.

"It'll help him get socialized," said Bruce, citing the kind of baby-book wisdom we used to spout with confidence back then, without knowing what any of it meant: what was a "socialized" baby anyway? Would he crawl around the room shaking hands?

It may have been a strange idea, continuing with a big party even after Jin made his long-delayed arrival, but we had promised ourselves that we would not give up enjoying our lives as adults when we became parents, as so many of our friends had done, vanishing into a world that began with infants who could never be left with babysitters and going on to endless tournaments of soccer and basketball. The wild optimism of new parents! We wouldn't quite manage to continue on just as before, either, but that knowledge lay ahead of us.

While Jin landed in our arms in Seattle, friends snuck into our house and put up balloons and "Welcome Home Jin" banners; we kept these up, adding birthday signs for our friend. In one of my endless consignment store outings I had found a tuxedo-style baby bib, complete with faux bow tie.

In the three days we waited for Jin, after the phone call and the fax giving us his arrival information, we made enormous amounts of party food, dips and canapés from vintage cookbooks, and froze it. It kept me occupied at a time when I really needed a backup obsession to get away from the big one. I had begun asking Bruce a barrage of less and less answerable questions.

"What if he cries and cries and never stops? What will we do?" Any male pronoun, at this point, had just one possible referent.

"He'll have to sleep sooner or later." For Bruce, who had no experience of babies whatsoever, to be the voice of reason now strikes me as hilarious, but he was.

I had a cat, Savannah, a slip of black-and-white nervousness who adored me and followed me around the house, sleeping with me, and whom I in turn adored. One night, right before Jin's arrival, Savannah purred in her usual spot on my breastbone and I turned to Bruce in bed, in a panic.

"What if I love Savannah more than the baby?"

He thought about this for a minute. "Then I guess you'll love Savannah more than the baby. You'll still love the baby. That's the main thing."

"Oh."

Of course, I did not love the cat more than the baby. I could never love anything more than I loved that baby, as it turned out, not to mention that babies are babies and cats are cats and we love them wholly differently. The point is, I was making problems out of my household animals. Even party planning was better than that.

I bought long gloves at a consignment store, and an old dress. During the party, we played big band CDs and slow-danced through the living room. Our friends held Jin, one after another, and he loved it, laughing and smiling and finally falling asleep in his tuxedo bib on Bruce's chest as they did some version of a waltz together.

"He's bonding with you," said Clare, a doctor.

We had taken Jin to the pediatrician for his first checkup, but I noticed Clare giving him a quick once-over, palpating his organs. ("He's very healthy," she said, and we beamed, as if we had anything to do with it.) Clare's own children, two daughters, were with her ex-husband that night.

Bruce and I were happy to throw that party, happy our friend

Pam had a lovely fortieth with the kind of party she'd wanted, but most of what we saw and felt that evening was ourselves, new parents, and Jin being waltzed around the room in our arms, discovering my hair, drowsing off. We eventually added these party photos, too, to his arrival scrapbook. All of the balloons and signs—"Happy Birthday! Welcome Home Jin!"—stayed on the walls or bumped the ceiling until they wilted to the floor. Our friends held Jin too, but we always took him back before too long, and didn't put him to bed until he clearly needed to sleep: late, as he still lived on Korean time.

That third day was the first time I remember Jin feeling entirely relaxed when we held him for such long periods. We spun shuffling around the room, ate food and drank the drinks—martinis, sidecars—and heard the music of the years of our own birth. The whole night had an aura of timelessness, or time reborn: the new baby, the years of our own infancy come back.

I wondered if my own parents, who seemed so distant from this kind of joy, had drunk sidecars to celebrate my or my brother's births, or ever put on this kind of big band music just to dance us around the apartment. Our lives then, in Elizabeth, were organized around stoops, the front steps of our four-unit apartment buildings where women sat and children got together to play. We often ran down the street together to a vacant lot, a patch of glass-glitter and weeds that we loved. Or we snuck into the cemetery across the street; it served as my brother's and my favorite play space, with its child-sized architecture and naked, easily understood sentiment and places to hide. As we ran around, women gossiped and colored their fingernails and gathered on the stairs of the stoops, groups generally ignored by my stiff and shy mother.

Over the coming years our own neighbors in Bellingham— most of whom we barely knew then—would become some of the most important people in our world, and many friends from our single days would drift away. We stood on the cusp of changes so large and startling we could never have imagined them, as I expect my mother and father could never have dreamed of becoming the people they are now. Bruce and I did manage, to some degree, to continue to enjoy our lives as adults: to have dates together, to continue on as writers, to have our own friends whom we see almost daily. But the notion that anything could stay the same proved wrong; we became different people, as our baby redrew the map of our world.

⟋

As Jin's babyhood unfolded and I sank into maternity leave, I found myself ignoring the need to clean the house and wash clothes while he napped, and instead rushed, as soon as I knew he was asleep, to the computer. I wrote page after page of prose after years of writing poetry. I wrote family history, as if someone threatened to extract it all from my head and I needed to get it down. I had an MFA in poetry writing and had published two books of poems. In the past I had written some prose poetry. Otherwise, the concept of writing prose, and particularly memoir and family story—which I continued doing, compulsively—had not really occurred to me.

I could not, at first, have explained why my writing changed so much. I told Bruce this manuscript would probably end up stuck in a drawer forever. I called my project "Susanne's folly."

The pages did not seem to me like the kind of writing I did or the kind of writing I felt any good at doing. Nor could I quite define my audience. I considered myself a lyric poet, not a storyteller. But the urge to tell stories—my own and my family's—came over me whenever I could make it to the computer, and the number of pages grew.

I don't know how to separate my mother's instincts from my writer's instincts—the two were inextricably connected, and still are—but I do recall how much this new person in my life, who held my eyes with such naked curiosity, filled me with the drive to record my stories. I wanted to leave him a record, a guide to my life that was now his, and get down on paper some of what it meant, as far as I could give it meaning, to have this strange gift of life. It's a gift that in a young child is so new and at times, so baffling.

I remember being a child myself in Elizabeth and going with my father down to Gould's, the candy store at the corner of my street. Gould's was, even for that time, old-fashioned, with bins and barrels of sweets: rough wood holding cellophaned, glimmering pastels. Our neighborhood in Elizabeth was almost entirely Jewish, with many Holocaust refugees. Given his age, Mr. Gould might well have been one of these, and if so, the passage from the camp to this island of shaped sugar and entranced children must have been a strange, I hope paradisical turn.

I loved Gould's. At the same time, the plenty laid out in the store often paralyzed me. My father would hold out a dime and the possibilities—candy cigarettes in their little mock carton, a handful of licorice, sugary gum wrapped in cartoons—were agonizing. I don't know why, on this particular occasion, the choice of what thrilling sweetness to put in my mouth jolted me into some new awareness of myself, embodied there. As I thought furiously about candy, I started thinking about thought itself. I suddenly couldn't imagine why my consciousness was there, why it alone held the universe inside itself—why the things of the world funneled down into this small, greedy thing called *me*. I was five or so, too young to realize that the universe funneled down into everyone else's mind in exactly the same way. It was not an aggrandizing thought but an awful one—my tininess, in light of the centrality my consciousness seemed to have in the world, made me ill.

"I don't know what I want," I said, or something to that effect, with a little sob. Then, "Why am I *here?*"

I recall my father's irritation, thinking, I'm sure, that I was asking why he had taken me to Gould's, when I no doubt had whined at him to go. And I had no idea how to phrase my question any differently so I expect I just repeated it, and then we left without candy.

❧

I began my rush into prose by writing the story of my grandfather from Barbados. He had come to the United States as a child with his mother, Berenda, after the death of his father.

My grandfather, Louis Charles Harry Clarke etc. (his full name was quite long), was the thirteenth child of a manic mother, manic even in her naming. After twelve children she still had not depleted her overabundance of names to bestow. There was a fourteenth child in the family but he had died of pneumonia, joining in death a sister who died after marrying and moving to Martinique, poisoned, my grandmother told me, by her mother-in-law, who wanted her son to marry a Catholic. Berenda had run out of money before coming to the US, though she left my grandfather here and went back to Barbados again and again.

I wrote Louis's story, getting from an aunt a family tree of the Barbados family, from historical journals the tale of the indentured servants sent to that island in exile from England after participating in the Monmouth Rebellion back in the 1600s. My mother had a box of old letters that had belonged to my grandfather, one from a cousin who'd moved to England from Barbados and who claimed that my grandfather and many of his siblings had sprung from a series of affairs my great-grandmother had with military men.

My grandfather, when he lived, spoke very little, like his daughter, my mother. When he did speak to us children, he talked about World War I. He had served for two countries in that war, with a serious injury from each stint: a bullet in the neck, then the loss of one and a half fingers. He also talked about Barbados. He spat out tales about someone named Hanging Judge Jeffreys and slapdash trials called the Bloody Assizes. When I read the history of the Monmouth Rebellion, I found out that most of the rebels—who aimed to unseat King James II in favor of James Scott, Duke of Monmouth, fearing that the Catholic James II would turn all of England back to Catholicism—had indeed been tried by a man named Jeffreys. Judge Jeffreys got his nickname from those trials, and their quick and public executions by hanging. And the trials were known as the Bloody Assizes.

My grandfather spoke of these things with the bitterness of recent history, with a personal bile, though the events had occurred three hundred years in the past. The histories also noted that only the lowest class of rebels was given the grace of being sent off as indentures to Barbados—essentially enslaved for life—rather than hung. My grandfather did not mention this.

It felt bizarre to understand my grandfather in retrospect as caught like a fly—wings spread but static—in the amber of this history. If I needed proof that our pasts can hold us captive if we're not careful, the proof was here. My mother's family had been defined in many ways by my grandparents'—especially my grandfather's—hatred of Catholics, a faith two of his normally obedient daughters married into. My aunt Kathleen eloped with her Catholic man, my Irish coal miner uncle Joe, at eighteen, vanishing one day and coming home a wife. Religious tensions arose at many family get-togethers and also strained my parents' marriage—my mother's having chosen a Catholic husband did nothing to stop her from developing the same intolerance of that religion—and probably did more than anything else to keep my father away from church.

"Absurd superstition," my grandmother would find a way to say about Catholicism as we sat around the Thanksgiving table, and my grandfather would be off on the group he always called "the bloody RCs [Roman Catholics]." My mother would agree with her parents; my father would be hurt.

And all of this stemmed from a long-dead conflict, a king who did not after all try to turn England Catholic again, a series of ancient and mostly forgotten lapses in judgment.

After writing all I could find about the Barbados family, I wrote the story of Holly Park, where my grandfather had built his cottages on Barnegat Bay in New Jersey. And I wrote the story of my summers there and the nuclear power plant and the secret toxic dump sites on local farms. It was the tale of my body and my miscarriage and the jagged shards of family history that catch in your throat and over time, if not extracted, choke you. It limned the part of me that exposed and reclaimed and rethought family, the part that felt drawn, from childhood, to adoption.

I didn't know this, but I was writing my first book of nonfiction prose, *Body Toxic: An Environmental Memoir*. I wrote in the epilogue to the book about Jin and his asthma—Jin had turned three by the time I got to the end of the book—and about one day when I brought him outside to paint. Jin had moved away from his easel and begun to paint the withering raspberry leaves a bright summer green. We both had this need, it seemed: to paint things, to revivify.

It seemed obvious to me, once the manuscript of this first book of prose came together, that Jin had turned me toward prose and that I did not, actually, feel unsure of my audience: I wrote for him. I wanted him to know our family history, for it to be his, even the parts of it that may not have been beautiful or even fathomable. I will never understand my grandfather, what he lived through, or his mad mother. But I wanted the stories to exist, fleshed out, expansive and clear, in a form this small person in his speckled painting smock and his brush, trying to lick new life onto the leaves, might be able to understand someday. I still wrote poetry and loved poetry. I wanted the capacity of the prose book to pack in whatever I had of my own Bloody Assizes and Hanging Judges and all the rest, to follow my own histories as far as I could and with facts, to keep me and most important, my son, out of that amber of confusion.

We fed Jin in our laps for months. We would feed him dinner, then put him into a bouncer attached to the doorjamb to giggle maniacally while we ate. When we'd eaten a bit we took him out of the bouncer and put him on our laps again, letting him eat off our plates. We had a hand-me-down high chair; we just never used it. It made Bruce uneasy. High chairs were too different from laps, which were themselves a world away from the chest hold of mostly bottle feedings, and well into the older baby realm of solid food. Time and growth were not my husband's friends. We argued about using the high chair and one day, when Jin was eight months old and had spilled his eggs on me for the hundredth time and Bruce was out of the house, I strapped baby Jin into it. He liked it. I laid out his eggs and tofu on the tray, and he shoveled palmfuls into his mouth, in between me spooning in careful bits. I gave Jin peas to practice his newly developing pincer grip and he threw them around the room as the dogs collided into each other to catch them in their mouths, something they never succeeded at though they seemed eager enough to die trying. Bruce walked in.

"No, don't do that!" he said, then, "Jin's growing up too fast."

Children do. They grow up far too fast and we can't stop them, and we simply have to haul out their metaphorical high chairs when we have had enough of wearing their metaphorical eggs on us.

Bruce reconciled himself to the high chair and we ate with Jin parked at the table. He babbled away and, in his new perch, developed a funny habit of pointing one index finger into the air while delivering a speech that came out as something like, "Abba dabba dabba DABBA!" waving his finger at us and chewing on each syllable like a politician or a preacher. Then he fixed us with a long look, as if to say, "There! That's what I think of your parenting up to now." Sometimes he would inject himself into a conversation or disagreement with up-spired finger and a string of syllables that ended on that firm note, looking at us with a definite "Well, that settles that" look.

There were times I felt quite certain that the baby knew exactly what we were saying, and that his practicing language had to do not with learning to express himself or understand us, but to help us catch up to some level of certainty about the world which he had already achieved himself. Perhaps in my rush of new writing I only sought to bring myself to his level of awareness. He seemed, at times, to know far more about things than I did.

When Jin made those babble speeches, we liked to pretend, while he throned it over us in his high chair, that he was President Bill Clinton or Clinton's press secretary Mike McCurry, and held wooden spoons up to his mouth as if they were microphones and peppered him with questions.

"What do you have to say about Monica Lewinsky?" we'd urge, in those days of the Clinton scandal, and, if we were lucky, we would get a waving finger and an "abba dabba" speech, which we of course interpreted to mean, "I did not have sex with that woman, Miss Lewinsky." Other times, Jin would give us the infant equivalent of an eye roll and a sigh: "Really? Must I? Again?" At times I got the feeling that my baby just pretended not to know everything that was going on around him.

"Really, Mom," he seemed about to say, catching my eyes with his calm stare while I fluttered over the job of cutting those tiny fingernails without sawing the flesh around them, "really, not such a big deal. I'll be doing it myself in no time, what with these opposable thumbs and all."

I have a personal horror of people who call their babies "old souls," maybe because, in the New Age world of the Pacific Northwest, statements like that often get followed by the speaker offering to show you her baby's past-lives regression chart, in which he was invariably Alexander the Great or Gandhi or somebody else famous and enviable. Still, babies seem to know things, like the times when my baby saw me crying after a too-long workday and no time to shower and no sleep, and touched his finger with incredible softness to the drop on my cheek, looking into my eyes.

"It's all right," I would tell him, as if he really meant to offer comfort.

There are moments, in parenting, when everything feels wrong. I had a conversation once with one of my cousins, when she said she had been walking her second child around the house all night while he cried, and as it was summer and hot, she kept circling around an open window.

"I suddenly realized that if I just threw him out it would all be over," she told me and we laughed, because though my cousin is a full-time mom and a conservative Christian who volunteers for Focus on the Family—things we do not talk about—we understand each other about moments like this. A thought like that flashes through all parents' minds at some point. We're horrified at ourselves and banish it instantly, but we still have it, that promise of an end to the baby crying and the grinding exhaustion.

And then come the moments when everything feels right, when the baby and you seem to read each other perfectly and agree it was all supposed to happen just like this, things moving along in their random way to reach this room, this soft rug, this game of itsy-bitsy spider.

We face and reface the question of why and how we're together, a wonder that's part of the creation of our family. Because of visa stalling in Beijing, which changed our application away from the first country we looked at, China. Because we happened to be home from a long trip to Siena, Italy, by July 29, when the referral came, though we'd been told no referral would come until August. So Jin could attend college, as he probably could not in Korea. So he could be treated for a dangerous allergy that has required years of expensive therapy. So I could tell my stories to someone for whom they would all, ultimately, be harmless—the family madness isn't his legacy—and make sense. Because life is random. Because things had turned out sadly for a young woman—and a young man, if he knew—back in Korea. Because, possibly, there are things we can do for one another.

Part II

BEFORE

3.

Dream Baby

COMING OF AGE as I did in the late 1960s and early 1970s, I remember the mystique that developed about the concept of birth bonding. I heard this belief echoed back then on television and the radio and in the advice of doctors like Frederick Leboyer and midwives like Ina May Gaskin. To do right by your children meant having them in pain and bonding to them the instant they emerged, as if we had not human infants but little ducks who would follow the first thing they saw, be it mother or forceps. I have no idea how much my own mother indulged in painkillers during labor—my guess would be that she went along with whatever her doctors wanted her to do—but motherhood as a necessary martyrdom fit her philosophy of life as a woman.

My cousin Mark, as a teenager, said that he would never let his wife have painkillers during labor.

"The babies don't bond," said Mark, "and then that's it." We never speculated on what *it* was.

Or perhaps I am wrong and my mother resisted painkillers;

she was a Christian Scientist till her marriage and never lost that church's suspicion of medicine. She breast-fed my brother and me in the bottle-and-formula 1950s, wanting to do things the better, modern way for her children. It may be that my mother's dutiful parenting tilted me toward adoption. She studied her Dr. Spock's baby book, and took us to checkups though it violated her beliefs, and fed us a nutritious diet, and saw to it that we had piano lessons, and all the time remained a million miles away. *It*, whatever it was, could happen with any mother and child.

In the late 1960s and early 1970s, all matters ideological tended to be loud, much debated, and larded with dogma and exaggeration. It did not seem extreme, from a 1960s perspective, to think that your first minutes on the planet would make or break the course of your life. Women began to minimize the presumed shock of the birth procedure for the sake of their infants, giving birth in tubs of warm water, with music, gritting their teeth to avoid the epidural anesthesia that might make the process less painful. At the same time, the Vietnam War fueled another wave of international adoption and the sexual revolution decreased adoptions at home. Then as now, many celebrities—Mia Farrow, Julie Andrews, among many others—adopted internationally, creating a public awareness of children from another country joining American homes.

Between the children who arrived in balletically orchestrated births and the children who might be found, homeless, in a war zone, without even a clear age, it was hard to see how the same result came out of it: a family. The divorce rate would soon skyrocket, peaking in the late 1970s at more than half of all marriages. The infants who slid into the world on a tide of warm water later treaded water accompanied by stepparents and stepsiblings—often multiple sets of them.

In the midst of this changing landscape of family, I thought of adoption. I also imagined pregnancy and birth, slipping out a child in a haze of pain that would be excruciating and romantic, and that this child would sense I endured for her sake. At times, that second option seemed the better one, the heady first moments of holding a child you grew inside you—though as I watched my aunts and cousins go through pregnancy, I never felt called on to carry a child myself. It had its own, possessed beauty, the mother-to-be with her hand permanently stuck to the shelf of her belly, as if the baby might vanish on her, with a face of pure abstraction. But with that grew the exhaustion, the legs that came to seem so weak and inadequate under that weight of infant.

My aunts and cousins on the Italian side of my family echoed that warning, explaining the physical toll it took to make a baby.

My aunt said of my cousin, pregnant at eighteen, "It's a boy. See how good she looks? They say if you're carrying a girl she'll drain the prettiness out of your face."

My cousin was married then. I told my father that I thought eighteen was awfully young to be a mother and he said, "What's wrong with it? You grow up with your children."

My father had a lot of little sayings like that, and this one, like most of them, made no sense to me; if you both were growing up, who made the decisions? Who knew what to do?

Somehow the image that stuck in my mind was a baby who preexisted any physical choices I might make, who clearly needed me. She wouldn't suck the prettiness, to the extent that it existed, out of my face. She couldn't come at me with the charge I leveled at my own parents throughout my teens: *Why the hell did you make me? I didn't ask for this.*

My dreams were, looking back, oversimplified and over-romantic. Did I imagine the birth mother? No, I'm embarrassed to say I did not, until I adopted my child and sank myself into her pain when I thought of losing him.

I pictured a girl. My mother had been ambivalent about raising a daughter; fine, I would correct that, by choosing a daughter.

My mother had been vocally ambivalent about children in general, though in her shy, brusque way she adored my brother. She loved to say that "not all women are cut out to be mothers," with a lift of the brow that indicated she might be in that company. She told us, when we asked why she had children, that my father wanted them. Like fathers of the era, though, mine was absent a lot of the time, including when we arrived on the scene; he was not even in the waiting room when I emerged, but wandering the hospital for some reason. He got into the elevator and the nurse pushed forward the scrap of a body in her arms—all in pink—and said, "This is your daughter."

The nurse recognized my father from a previous glimpse of him at my mother's bedside. My father had no idea I'd even been born, or—in those days before ultrasound—that I would be a girl.

He says he remembers being happier than he was at the birth of my brother, I think because labor happened so fast with me that he had no time to worry. My mother, on the other hand, reported that her pregnancy with me happened by accident, and she did not in any case want a daughter.

"Women want boys," was another one of her raised-brow sayings. When someone who had a girl went on to have a boy, she would say something like, "Well, I bet she's happy about that!"

The love of boys was a running theme in my mother's family, which tended to produce more girls than boys. In my generation, we had six girl cousins to two boys, my brother Chris and my cousin Mark. I saw far more of the people on this side of my family than those on my father's; we spent most holidays together and much of the summer. In 1930 my grandfather and his cousin John, also from Barbados, built the summer places known in the family as the Big Bungalow and the Little Bungalow or the Big Cottage and the Little Cottage. My grandfather built these places—not much more than shacks—for his wife and four children, who promptly took to leaving him for the entire summer. My grandmother May spent very little time with my grandfather, also traveling solo during much of the rest of the year. She told me once when I was a teenager that she'd tried to break off her engagement with my grandfather, but her mother wouldn't let her return the ring.

We rarely dignified the bungalows with the name of *houses*. The so-called Big Bungalow had a toilet, a tiny galley kitchen, no hot water, and two bedrooms plus a porch with pullout beds. The Little Bungalow had two bedrooms and a shower that did have hot water; we put this bathroom in during my childhood and I helped with the plumbing. We cousins—there were eight of us—were a mobile workforce down at the shore. We pumped bilge on my uncle Joe's boats, washed the decks, and if we were girls, also did the dishes, heating water on the stove. We painted the cottages when they needed painting, even brushed lung-scalding copper bottom paint on the boats.

My uncle Joe had been born into an immigrant Irish coal mining family in western Pennsylvania. At ten he had been forced into the mines to work; at sixteen, he ran away from home to escape mining and joined the merchant marine. He'd learned to sail and still loved it as an adult, buying sailboats and fixing them up. He worked as a machinist.

We kids, mostly Chris and me and my cousins Helen and Mark, learned to sail from our uncle and sailed on our own, too. We did the riskiest things we could think of when we went out in the boat unsupervised: sailed in storms though our mast would tend to draw lightning, sailed into the wind with the boat so far over the keel stuck out of the water and one of us would occasionally tumble overboard. I'm still not sure how we managed to do all of these things—at least, the thunderstorm sails—without drawing down on ourselves the wrath of the elders. I think down at the shore our parents got preoccupied with their chatter and their gin and tonics and didn't really notice what we did. Or perhaps, for my mother and her siblings at least, the place where they had been children took them back to a negligent and childlike state, playing cards together and gossiping a bit, laughing softly.

We sat on the roof of the Little Bungalow at night, looking at the stars and arguing about things like natural childbirth.

My brother and I and my mother spent many weeks during the summer down at the shore. My father took his vacation days there, and even when he had to stay in northern New Jersey and work, we would often go for a few weeks and he'd join us on the weekends. We went down to the shore while we lived in our Elizabeth apartment, and after that, when my father bought his first small house just outside of Elizabeth. I slept in the back bedroom of the Big Cottage, a room with two sets of bunk beds always filled with some grouping of my girl cousins. Helen and I decorated the back bedroom, since we were the oldest girls, according to our whims of the moment, so the room went from Barbies to Monkees posters to Monty Python.

Once, when I was alone in the Big Cottage—everyone else had gone crabbing or something, but I'd opted out—my grandfather called me.

"Come *here*," he half screeched; the tone of his voice sounded strange, and wrong to me somehow. I was ten.

It was the middle of the day. I looked for my grandfather and found him in one of the bottom bunks in the back bedroom.

"Come *here*," he said again and pulled the sheet down. He was naked. He gestured toward me in a way that repulsed me; his hand stuck out, the one hand of his that had all five fingers, frantic, and greedy. He started toward me and I ran into the middle bedroom, a room with a blue door and an ancient lock you pressed down with your thumb. I locked the lock and did not come out until I heard my brother's voice.

Susanne Antonetta

I knew, without quite having language for the knowledge, that if I ever tried to tell my parents what had happened I would get into terrible, terrible trouble, both for lying and for something else that I couldn't put my finger on, a guilt that could obtain to you for making someone else want to do something that was wrong. To be in trouble for both was a paradox but I could feel it, as I'd once sensed I should not ask my mother what the word *rape* meant, but did anyway. She was making the bed. She stopped and pulled the sheet up then with an arm that snapped with anger.

"It means *attack*," she said. "Now get out of here. Don't let me hear you use that word again."

I told my brother Chris about my grandfather, and Chris stayed close to me for years after that, and I never got anywhere near my grandfather again unless plenty of family members were around.

What I did not think about at the time, but did later, were the implications of this incident for my mother: her dislike of women, her deep ambivalence about having a daughter, her recoiling at the simplest touch. I have no idea what may have happened to her as a child, though I can guess she would have been far more vulnerable than her daughter if someone tried to hurt her.

I think for my mother, as for me, in spite of what may have happened there, the shore cottages were the closest thing in our lives to a true home, the place where our child selves explored and took risks and learned to be one of many, and where our adult selves, such as they were, formed out of the chaos.

In 1966, when I was ten, the National Organization for Women was founded. Four years later, that organization and feminists like Gloria Steinem and Betty Friedan floated the then-strange argument that women might choose not to have children at all. True, the Pill had been on the scene for a while, but never have children? We saw motherhood the way boys our age saw getting a job—as a burden no one could opt to put down. To consider how and when to have children seemed a heady enough freedom. The other new consideration for us girls—that we might, tentatively and so as not to inconvenience the men in our lives, get a job—brought another twist in what we thought we understood about our lives. It was scary and intoxicating.

I had been raised to think my future would be marriage and stay-at-home motherhood, the template for the life of my mother and my father's mother. My mother's mother was a little different, though she had worked only when forced by circumstance, as she was during the Great Depression, when she opened a boardinghouse. An Englishwoman from the town of King's Lynn in Norfolk, she came to the US as a war bride of the First World War, having nursed my grandfather, who had gone from being a British citizen (Barbados was then a British colony) to a Canadian to an American, fighting under the first two flags.

My grandmother proved to be a true product of a port town that had produced some of history's best-known travelers, including the explorer George Vancouver, who mapped my future home place of the Pacific Northwest for the Crown, and the mystic Margery Kempe. My grandmother traveled constantly, going alone on safari at the age of seventy-nine. In Kenya she slept in treetops and watched Masai tribesmen harvest and drink cow's blood. I remember her delight in the way they milked blood from the cows' jugular veins, "just enough," she said, "not to kill the animal, and really very nutritious." She remained this restless and fearless person into her eighties, when she sank into an equally ferocious dementia.

One of my mother's sisters, my aunt Kathleen, had an early memory of sitting on the front steps and crying because her mother had gone off somewhere. My mother never complained about her mother's absences, and generally there was no love lost between them. My grandmother fulfilled her part of the social contract by bearing children, never taking a job unless she had to, and doing the expected things when she was home, like cooking.

My mother always made my future clear to me, though we did not talk much. She was not one to say much of anything—she was a silent person, like her father. If she says anything, it tends to come in the form of pronouncements.

My aunts chimed in with the vital business of fitting us girls—the six cousins—to our expectations. "You look for a man who wants to take you home," I remember an aunt of mine saying as she sat at her country-style kitchen table in her boxy suburban house, licking color over her fingernails with a brush. "If he's serious he'll want to show you off. A man heading into business."

This aunt had been born on a tiny island in Greece and

had emigrated here as a child with her then-poor family. Like so many ethnic Americans, she remade herself in the nowhere-and-everywhere style of our culture: she became a Methodist, a maker of casseroles, a woman with Middle Eastern carpets and Early American furniture and Wedgwood, a stay-at-home mother. She liked to warn us off premarital sex by saying, "No man will buy the cow if the milk is free," so often that when we were older, my brother's live-in girlfriend, Barb, used to eye me and moo when my aunt came into the room.

This same aunt told riddles to pass the time: in one, a boy's father rushes him to the emergency room after an accident and the surgeon says, "I cannot operate on him, he's my son."

"Who is the surgeon?" asked my aunt. She gave us a day to come up with the answer but, stumped, my girl cousin and I never did. "The surgeon was the boy's mother," my aunt finally told us, and we stared at her: absurd.

At sixteen I joined the National Organization for Women. I was a high school dropout with a drug problem—I used LSD and heroin and downs, and many types of speed, separately or all at once, all day every day. It was an inexplicable move for a person like me, and one I still can't make sense of. I thumbed rides to the meetings—I thumbed rides everywhere, never looking before getting into the car, and occasionally had to jump out of a car at a red light when the driver clearly had something in mind. Several of these men, usually the ones whose sweat-reek stung like ammonia, gunned their engines and sped past the NOW street as I asked them over and over to make the turn—or hell, just let me out—barely braking for lights and leaving me to fling myself from the car when it slowed. Then I would arrive at meetings with holes in my jeans, torn knees and fresh bruises, to discuss sexual assault as coercion and a tool of the patriarchy. I loved NOW and never thought of what happened to me on the way there as having any relationship to the talks, which were done in a circle, though I listened and never participated.

I once, inexplicably, dragged my mother along with me to a NOW meeting. I assume I was sober then and that she drove us, or perhaps I did. I only remember forming that circle with my mother sitting beside me, looking even more uncomfortable than usual. Her discomfort thrummed in my direction, making me feel ridiculous. I suspect—since I recall a few NOW conversations about cosmetics mildly embarrassing me—that I went to NOW meetings in my full *Jersey Shore* Snooki makeup, part of my uniform in those years. The NOW women's criticism of makeup hadn't bothered me much before; I felt invisible. But a physical awareness of my mother, a tiny woman in her uniform of sensible black shoes with nylon stockings, permed hair, and housedress, made me cringingly aware of myself. The women at NOW, whatever their age, had long, straight hair (straightening it, for many, was no doubt their one undetectable vanity), no makeup, and jeans. Our discussion leader sat down.

"Now," she burst out brightly, "all of the women here who have faked orgasms, raise your hands!"

Every woman in the room other than us raised her hand. I had in fact faked orgasms by then, but couldn't bring myself to declare in front of my mother that I not only had had sex— which I'm sure she'd figured out on her own—but was enough of a sexual sophisticate to fake things. My mother stared with painful seriousness at her shoes. The women in jeans looked at us for a long moment, then the discussion moved on to the specifics of sexual frustration. I never talked my mother into going anywhere new and strange with me again.

I stayed with NOW, ringing doorbells and arguing for the Equal Rights Amendment, which never passed. I said: It will be good for your daughters, for equal pay, equal education. I wanted the ERA for my own daughters, the daughters I would choose, who would proudly bring me to meetings of whatever political cause captured their attention, who would be able to answer that riddle. I did end up with a child who answered it, as thoughtlessly as I would have liked—but not a girl child, and not from where I expected.

When, in my imagination, I saw an adopted child, I did not think much about what circumstances might have led to the baby's adoption. It was not a fantasy of rescuing a child, but a pull toward a particular type of bond. A strange beauty, already formed and just forming, mine to hold for a while.

My parents fueled this desire in their different ways. My mother seemed to feel betrayed by her own body, both in producing a child of the wrong sex and in producing children who—much as she adored my brother—had somehow occluded her. She made a great deal of fuss over my brother's left-handedness, which was hers too, and his eye color, a hazel that came closer to her gray-blue than my dark eyes did, but, as a woman who never topped five feet, with an equally tiny bone structure and light hair, she saw in our tall, broad, Latin selves not a legacy but an overwriting of herself.

"What happened to my genes?" she used to wail, looking at us, before she developed dementia.

I bear a resemblance, at least in my father's eyes, to his mother, a good Catholic housewife who had four children and made caring for them her life. My father wanted badly to identify me with her.

"You're like my mother," he used to say if I did anything remotely feminine: cooked, or played with one of my little cousins. But I was not, and I am not, and that became clearer over the years. I threw my adolescence away on drugs, came home at all hours or not at all. I joined NOW, which was more socially acceptable than getting high but equally mysterious to my father.

"What do they talk about?" he used to ask, and then answer himself with, "a lot of whining."

At seventeen I cleaned my system out of drugs, inadvertently, after a week of desperate sickness following an overdose of street methadone. At nineteen, I went door-to-door handing out literature for a group called Zero Population Growth, earnestly explaining the dangers of adding more children to a crowded planet. I got a GED, went to community college, and transferred to Oberlin. It made my father happy that I finally went to college, but my focus on women's writing and feminism grated on him.

"Those girls," he said, a term that encompassed students and professors and women like Gloria Steinem, whom he saw in the news, "are never going to be happy."

I married relatively young. I met my husband in my junior year of college, in our senior year we began dating, and we moved in together after graduation and never lived apart again. I was engaged by the age of twenty-four. My father loved my husband, but found my system of splitting up household chores baffling and worrying. I was not his mother. If it wasn't my turn to do the dishes, they sat in the sink. My father predicted a grim future for me: Bruce walking out to pursue a woman who would not leave dishes in the sink and not be a whiner.

"I don't know about you," he said, echoing one of my mother's favorite expressions: "I don't know about you, Susanne."

What? I used to ask my mother now and again, back when she could remember what she had just said. "What don't you know about me?"

And she'd say, "I just don't know."

Which is, perhaps, my point. Biology to me always smacked a little of bait and switch.

⌒

I have a bit of my grandmother in me: I travel, spend money I do not have to go to places just for the experience of it. My cousin Olivia and I have a joke: there are two kinds of Cassills (the surname on my mother's side of the family), those who do nothing but travel, and those who never go anywhere. I fall into the former category. For my parents, especially my mother, these legacies I have are far from lovable. Without biology, I imagined there could be a cleaner love: no overidentification that could turn into bitter reminders, as in the case of my mother, or frustration, as in the case of my father.

I had a fantasy of being adopted myself when I was a child, fueled by a lack of baby pictures of me. I tried to imagine who my lost biological mother and father might be and if I'd ever meet them. It was an unsustainable fantasy, unsustainable in light of how everyone who met my family remarked on how much I resemble my father.

It amused me to read, as an adult, studies that identify an adoption-fantasy stage as developmentally normal. It occurs to most children between the ages of six and ten, when they picture their "real" parents as everything their actual parents are not. I have not read any studies addressing how children who know they're adopted handle this phase, though I know that adopted children tend to fantasize birth parents who are extremes—either poor, even criminal parents, or rich celebrities or nobility. Theirs is a longing, I guess, suffused with the anxiety of all that could really be true.

My mother's side of the family put a great deal of weight on biology. One of my aunts frequently talked about people coming from "bad stock." In that family, "You don't know what you're getting" was a common response to adoption, as if children are random things you snag up with one of those claws at a video arcade, and when you reach into the stuff of your own and another's DNA you do know what you're getting.

After one of these conversations about the discredited stock of my cousin's wife, I told my aunt that I doubted my own stock was much better.

"No," she said after a long pause. "Your genes are pure."

My aunt talked about *genes* and *stock* a lot.

Looking back, I can't imagine what my aunt was talking about: my genes derived, immediately, from three different countries—Italy, England, and Barbados—and plenty more in the distant past. My extended family was full of people who'd been flamboyantly mentally ill: fire starters, manics, gloomy depressives like my grandfather from Barbados. He descended from Redlegs, former white slaves who formed one of the most despised classes on the island. "All Creoles are crazy," a Trinidadian friend of mine once told me; to be Creole in the Indies means you can trace your descent back to a European country, but in a family line that has been on the island for many centuries, there are always plenty of other lines of descent in the mix: Portuguese Jewish, Native, no doubt African. I think my friend implied that those who kept their skin fairly pale in the Caribbean did so by inbreeding. Maybe my aunt had her own doubts about my stock, and was trying to spare my feelings.

Meanwhile, I developed my own sense of biological connection. I became the family cook, starting at around age twelve. Actually, I had known the joys of feeding people since I got my first Suzy Homemaker oven and made chocolate cake hockey pucks for my brother, who loved them. By the time I hit my tweens, my mother had grown tired of her housewife routine, which she had thrown herself into since the births of my brother and me. It was a thankless role, and my family had become dead-locked over the years in the area of food.

My brother and I favored the Italian dishes my mother had learned to make, early in her marriage, from my father's sister Philomena. We lapped up anything with pasta and tomato sauce and couldn't stand her preferred British cuisine of well-cooked beef roasts and lamb. When she cooked what she liked, I took the smallest cube of meat I could get away with, coating it on each side with a thick crust of black pepper to make it palatable and, I'm sure, making obnoxious comments. My father loved Italian food too, and my mother gave in to us by cooking Italian a great deal but retaliated by declaring that anything Italian upset her stomach. She made our spaghetti and tomato sauce and sat at the table with a slice of cold ham, sighing out her martyrdom at having nothing to eat.

When I started cooking at twelve, I cooked awful things: Hamburger Helper, chicken pieces shoved in the oven with pota-toes. Still, it broke the family stalemate. My brother and I would both eat what I cooked, even if it didn't taste very good. Chris often wandered into the kitchen while I worked and threw his own idea of the right seasonings into the pot. We ate, I suspect, largely out of curiosity. My father ate so that he wouldn't discour-age me from the one feminine thing I liked to do.

I loved the chemistry of cooking. I also loved such a physical, primal form of nurture. I did not feel close to my family, except my brother, but I felt close, at least for the moment, to everyone

I fed. The beauty of food was that you gave someone a gift that formed their substance.

When Jin arrived, I took to my small kitchen and cooked and pureed all manner of foods, freezing portions in ice cube trays for his meals, of sweet potato and quiche filling and peas. Bruce and I developed a system: one yellow vegetable cube and one green vegetable cube and one protein for each meal. I did not yet know who my baby Jin and I would be together, but I knew I wanted to be part of him, touch him at his inmost—his cells and his dreams and the tiny pipettes of blood that nourished his brain and his heart. I did not give him my ancestors, an absence signaled daily by his striking and different features, and one for which I became, daily, more and more grateful. I loved his developing and unimplicated body. I knew that the food I gave him and the sleep I helped him into would make him, every day, grow into himself.

4.

An Empty Car Seat

MY FIRST EXPERIENCE of motherhood, or near-motherhood, was pregnancy. Bruce and I had started trying for children in our early thirties, after debating adoption versus pregnancy for a long time. Put together, we had a genetic picture that looked like a Munch painting: bipolar disorder and alcoholism going back many generations. I flew to Barbados at the age of twenty to meet my family there; I traveled with a cousin on that side of the family, who later would be unable to conceive a child. There we learned our line was "crazy crazy," and the man who told us this (our second cousin George) exposed his penis to us as he said it. George was about sixty, scrawny, and naked; the penis curled in a little bottle like a fetal pig. An invalid, he used the bottle as a crude catheter, and he shifted his sheets constantly, restlessly. What souls would swim upstream to our wombs?

Bruce's father, we knew, had had a nervous breakdown during the war and had been sent home. The family story was that he had seen terrible things in combat. But we got his war records from the Marines and discovered he had been given a psychiatric release not long after enlisting, before active duty. He did not follow up with further psychiatric treatment, and became a drunk. Was it bipolar disorder or possibly schizophrenia? Two of my cousins on my father's side are schizophrenic, and we have no idea which side of their family passed on that gene.

This led to potential-parent conversations such as, "Well, if your father really *was* bipolar, the chances of our child having it could be fifty percent. If not, twenty-five percent." We could not quite decide what, even if those percentages proved reliable, that meant for us as parents. It can be difficult to have these disorders, but, in my experience, bipolar disorder has its gifts. I had been diagnosed with it around the age of thirty, though, like many people with that diagnosis, I struggled with misdiagnoses for a long time before that—I was considered an on-and-off depressive for much of my earlier life, even schizophrenic. I spent a lot of time in my twenties searching for the right medication; I didn't find it until I was in my first year of graduate school. Over time and with counseling, the medication became more and more successful. I am still bipolar but I can manage the mood swings and understand when to get help.

Bruce and I doubted we could afford adoption, since we were starting our first real jobs with a lot of debt. We each worked half-time so we could write, putting our income in the mid–five figures, while we lived in one of the most expensive parts of the country. We earned per year not much more than what some people told us we would need for adoption fees.

Mostly, I feared that, as a woman with bipolar disorder and a history of drug use, I would be rejected as an adoptive mother. I could not imagine that, in what always sounded like an irrational and arduous process, I would not be weeded out. I know a woman, the mother of my sister-in-law, who as an infant was left, wrapped in blankets, in a basket on her adoptive mother's doorstep during the Great Depression. I know another woman whose pregnant student came and asked her to adopt her baby. I began to have fantasies of these things: it seemed that if the birth mother chose you, no one else would say no. But nothing magical happened, and the thought of a rejection—did they call? write?—felt unbearable. All we needed to do to get pregnant was to have sex. That no one else could weigh in on. That we could do.

I went off the Pill and after a little over a year I went on a silent retreat, to a cloister in Vancouver. It had beautiful gardens with statues of Mary and the saints. I sat under them on benches and they looked down on me and seemed to make eye contact and offer something, as they were carved to do. My period was several days late; no big deal. Then I went to talk to a young nun for a session of spiritual direction and found myself choking with sobs.

"What's wrong," the pretty nun said. "What's wrong with your spiritual life?"

I said, "I don't know. I guess I wish women could be priests."

Then I added, "That's not really it. I think I'm just pregnant."

"You don't have to say that," she told me confidentially. "I know how you feel. All this him-him he-he-he. It gets to you. It gets to us too."

When I got home I almost vomited at the sight of dirty dishes in the dishwasher, and then I peed on a stick.

I loved pregnancy, something I had never imagined I would. I had just the first trimester and I suppose it didn't last long enough to get tiresome; even the nausea came as a signal flare from the brave new world. No looking at what had been dirtied for this new little life, whose eyes had only my eyes to see, my nose to filter odors, my burning throat to say "no" through. I loved the absentminded tiredness, the way I felt as if someone had lit a small, friendly fire, like a campfire, inside me. I still miss it. Like most wishes, this one is illogical; part of me would like to have had a full pregnancy and given birth to exactly the child I have, who is Korean.

At the end of the first trimester, I miscarried—after the period during which I'd been told miscarriages tend to happen. Bruce and I flew to Atlanta for the funeral of his grandfather, Big Gay (so-called to distinguish him from Bruce's oldest sister, Gay). Bruce's parents, both alcoholics, were dead by the time he was twenty, and Big Gay served as everyone's parent figure after that: loving, very eccentric. He watched *American Gladiators* and fretted about conspiracies—he thought at one point that Mary Tyler Moore and Brooke Shields were part of a "new breed of people" taking over the planet—while we brought him food, fitted him into a wheelchair, finally moved him into a home.

It was Halloween and skeleton pins jangled on the jackets of our flight attendants. "Trick or treat," they said, pouring out weak, scorched coffee.

The day after we landed, I doubled over. My sister-in-law,

trying to get herself and her three young children dressed for the wake, landed the job of making phone call after phone call to get me an appointment with a gynecologist.

I finally saw an old Southern doctor with a pinched face. He did an ultrasound with a portable machine, then ushered Bruce and me into his office with a bit of ceremony and talked about what was happening to someone named *her*. He addressed only Bruce, as if perhaps Bruce had gotten himself both female and pregnant at the same time.

"I'll tell you what I'm not seeing, I'm not seeing a heartbeat," he said, then, "Perhaps she miscalculated the date this pregnancy started. There's a small chance. She'll have to follow up at home."

I hated that doctor. I hated, irrationally, *her* too.

My pregnancy had been a multiple pregnancy, I learned from further ultrasounds. Bruce and I desperately wanted those babies, but I felt a strange lack of loss after the miscarriage, a floating. Occasionally I saw twins or triplets in strollers and became alive to my babies' absence, as if this mother passing in the mall had taken them from me. It was not precisely a sad feeling, more like a sense of some small ripple in the fabric of materiality, something that should have happened but didn't, quite. They passed. I passed. My gynecologist kept wondering how I was doing and giving me sticky notes with the names of support groups.

"You are grieving," she told me. "It's normal. Get some help with it."

She seemed certain of this. I took her sticky notes and imagined I was, in some way, grieving. I felt disturbed about what had happened in my body; it had seemed so ready to do this thing. I

discovered that my uterus was split into two chambers, one func-
tioning, one dim and cloistered off. This malformation had not
caused the miscarriage, but made pregnancy half again less likely.
It felt shameful to fail my husband, even my parents, like this.

I also know—and knew then—that I would not have chosen
that time to have a baby. We had just moved, the month I got
pregnant, from one coast to the other, to a strange town where
we had no friends. I was uncertain about the future of my work;
I did not have a steady job. I would have grieved, I imagine, for
my freedom, the chance to establish myself as a writer, a teacher,
to create a support network, before the overwhelming job of
parenting began.

We tried to conceive for a few more years, on the medical
advice that if it happened once it should happen again. I'm not
sure why we let the process go on so long. Neither of us felt we
needed to have biological children. I found pregnancy unbeliev-
able: not even the pink strokes on the stick I'd peed on finally;
not the promise of a heartbeat that wasn't my own, a thrumming
antiphone inside.

We researched various ways to adopt. First we looked into domestic adoption, which can be public—from the foster care system—
or private, a term usually used to mean working through an
agency and being selected by the birth mother to raise her child.
We agreed we did not care to stipulate race. Beyond that, the
world of adoption went from clear (baby needs parents/baby gets

parents who want baby) to overwhelming as soon as we began to look into it.

I called an agency in Washington, one that works with hard-to-place children (generally older children or those with medical needs), and talked to a woman who was pleasant and helpful but dropped, midway through the conversation, the fact that the first two of her adoption attempts had fallen through. In one case, the birth mother changed her mind (which happens about half the time, though generally before the infant is placed with adoptive parents) and in the next, the courts had changed theirs, returning a child to a birth mother whose rights had been terminated due to neglect.

"It was awful at the time but it's okay now," said the woman, who had finally adopted successfully.

I was reeling after that conversation. I knew, abstractly, that adoptions could fall through. But for it to happen again and again? To the same person? The woman had said that her experience wasn't too unusual.

Bruce and I talked about special needs, even about adopting an HIV-positive baby. Back in graduate school at the University of Virginia, I had gone to a talk by Dr. Elisabeth Kübler-Ross, the doctor known for her theory on the five stages of grief, about children born with the HIV virus in their system. She had been working with them at one of her clinics and talked about how, with plenty of physical contact and love, they often became HIV-negative.

We had been prepared for bureaucracy, home visits, paperwork. On the other hand, we live in a world in which millions of children literally or effectively have no parents. Adoption had seemed a process rife with frustration and long waits, but not loss; now we had to consider that possibility too. Could we parent a child who might remain seriously ill? Could we take a chance on a birth mother reversing her decision? The intake forms—with lists and lists of boxes where you check what you can or cannot accept in a child, from gender to disfigurement to major disability—felt like they were, and I suppose were in some sense, taking an inventory of our souls. We considered what we could and could not bear, how long we could expect to live and care for a child who would remain dependent. Some issues were lumped into phrases: "minor special needs" meant cleft palate or another correctible problem; "major special needs" could mean HIV or Down syndrome. We reported on ourselves on these intake forms: selfish people who could parent transracially but not face severe, as opposed to minor, health problems.

Sunny, an acquaintance in Bellingham who adopted from foster care, mentioned her caseworker's remark that adopting an HIV-positive child would mean scaling back her work hours, or quitting. "Handling HIV medication alone is a full-time job," Sunny told me. So we considered our time as well as our psychic resources, all of which felt like a betrayal of the babies we read about, all of whom deserved any sacrifice we might have to make. Except that we knew we could not make all those sacrifices and still be good parents. The moral yardstick reached its limit and gave us back a measure of ourselves.

"I've lost my parents," Bruce said one day. "I'm not sure I need more loss in my life."

We finally decided on an overseas adoption. I had become worried by the thought of an adoption being reversed. My choice wasn't a judgment on the rights of birth mothers or a vote on where children belonged, simply an honest appraisal of what I could handle emotionally. Of course, children don't come with guarantees, and loving a child means taking on the risk and the burden of that worst of all possible losses. But I didn't want to start out the process with the odds stacked against me.

We planned to adopt a little girl from China. Waves of information about the number of girls in Chinese orphanages, a by-product of that country's one-child policy and the expense of having a girl, had hit the news. We'd educated ourselves a great deal about the situation in China, met families with daughters from that country, chosen an agency and found a support group providing language and cultural education for us in our town. We live twenty miles from the border with British Columbia, which has a high Chinese population and would be rich in resources for our soon-to-be child. Our decision felt *right*, completely. We chose potential names, ones that worked in both languages.

Then our social worker called. Beijing, always unpredictable, had frozen the visa process for the foreseeable future. There were, however, boys in Korea. They didn't have enough parents for these boys. Did we want to switch our application to that country?

It all seems simple now. With a baby in need, we could stop

parsing out what we could and couldn't do and end the moral inventory each step in our process seemed fraught with. But we had the support group, the picture of little girls in orphanages in our heads. The names we juggled—Jade, or May. For unclear reasons, the majority of adoptive parents choose girls—perhaps a bit of bloodline sensitivity when it comes to males, perhaps a sense that adopted boys are likelier to be difficult. Parents seek girls to the point that, in Korea at least, boys have been considered special needs infants at times. Holding out for the girl we had imagined would mean waiting without a clear end in sight, while boys in Korea needed parents.

"Boys are nice too," said our social worker, Bill, an avuncular and commonsense guy who was close to retirement. He had a spray of graying moustache and an arch way about him that proved comforting. We thought about boys and their niceness. We switched countries.

We had just returned home from five months in Italy, working, when we got a phone message from Bill saying that he had mailed us a referral for a little boy. I forget which one of us called Bill back, but he acted like nothing much out of the way had occurred and promised we would get the referral packet the next day.

"You have the weekend to decide whether to accept this referral," he said.

"Decide," I said, staring at the phone, or Bruce, or both.

It had never struck me that we really, truly had anything to do with it. I suppose we had been told we could accept or reject referrals multiple times, but receiving one comes to feel so wanted and unlikely it's hard to imagine being handed a photo and asked to make a choice. The packet felt like our version of delivery: a tiny photograph slipping out of the envelope like the head of our baby crowning. Much dark hair and large liquid eyes surveying the photographer with curiosity but no surprise—a look we'd come to know. The random collection of information in Jin's file read like a novelist's starting notes. Birth mother: heart-shaped tattoo, waitress. Birth father: good at math. Birth grandmother: a shaman. These notes were all we had. Frozen after all this waiting, we went to a rock-and-driftwood beach and walked, holding hands.

We sat between the stag ends of the driftwood.

"A shaman. That's a good sign," Bruce said. We so wanted to be signaled; you and this baby will be right for each other.

Bruce and I backtracked and discovered where we'd been when our baby was born: Capri, Italy, in the Hotel Caesar Augustus, a magnificent but dilapidated place where many of the rooms had no running water but ours did. That, we decided, was a good sign too.

We put the tiny referral photo on our refrigerator. I knew I would love this boy, though I tried to compare this mystery with the mystery of a swelling stomach, a flutter deep in the pelvis. With pregnancy I had imagined my love for my baby growing as my stomach grew, my feet vanishing under its new importance. Here instead we had the six-week-old baby taped up in his look of solemn surprise. My touching, talking to, and kissing that picture couldn't bring him closer, in that growing, intestinal way. In fact, as we waited for his three-times-delayed arrival, Jin's photo seemed to shrink into the world of the refrigerator, with its notices of dentist's appointments, postcards from Greece, phone numbers of furnace repairmen.

My body gave me help in expecting Jin's arrival. My hormones changed, in the way they did during my three months' pregnancy. I cried at everything. Still, part of me wanted something more tangible to remind me of all the rest that was changing, a stomach you could put your hand on like a ledge of furniture. Something more than the car seat we bought from Target, waiting empty for us to put a new baby in it, and a blurred, serious photo, two inches around.

Waiting for Jin brought visions of a radically changed future: a baby in the house, a teenager, an adult child, even grandchildren. I became haunted—especially waking up in the dim, tepid early hours of the morning—by my younger, self-destructive self. I wondered if there was any chance I would raise a child like myself, and if I could stand that. I realized, while waiting for Jin to come, that I had never quite dropped the idea of suicide; I kept it in my head, always, my final consolation, my get out of jail free card, one I imagined playing if this-and-this-and-this in my life failed to get better. It had become a way of resolving those what-ifs that seem to rise and sink with the night and the moon: what if my husband dies, what if I never write again. It was born out of an emotional laziness, a way to end these fathomless speculations. With another life dependent on my own, to some extent, as long as I lived, I had to make a new pact with existence; I could not choose to exit it on my own terms any longer.

Unlike when we were expectant biological parents, we

agonized not about the infant's well-being (I remembered all the ultrasounds, triple-screens, amnios you undergo during pregnancy, monitoring the baby's health) but about our well-being. We knew his strength—his readiness—better than we knew our own. He would be, most likely, physically fine and well cared for at his arrival, and given how carefully babies get monitored before flight, if anything did go wrong, we would know and be prepared for it. Who would we be? We had cared for children in our family, particularly our nieces and nephews on Bruce's side, but we had never had a child in our house for more than a few days, and now we would be, forever, parents.

My own mother had found motherhood a role she had no instincts for, a fact she loved to amplify if anyone brought up the concept of maternal instinct. "What a bunch of bunk," she liked to tell me. "They're no fun, the little tykes." My mother had been prone to stare if a child—her own or anyone else's—took a fall and lay howling, rather than trying to help, and could not bring herself to give physical affection. I know some part of her wanted to be a good mother; the muscles wouldn't work. What, I wondered, could I expect for myself, her daughter?

On top of these questions came the questions posed by adoption itself. How would we bond with this baby, and how would the child ultimately judge us for choosing him, bringing him to this place, this home, rather than ceding him to another? The narrative of a biological child works on the cause and effect of the body and DNA, and the inexorability of the new life falling into the hands of the givers of its raw materials at birth, at least in our culture. In India or other cultures that accept reincarnation, karma and caste form a narrative for the specifics of the where and why of a child's arrival. In our culture, my family would have to create a narrative of its own. I heard of research like that in Nancy Verrier's book *The Primal Wound* or the psychologist Marshall Schechter's influential 1960 paper "Observations on Adopted Children," which argued that adopted children were far more prone to problems than biological children, though when I looked into these sources later I discovered that both were highly anecdotal and built on poor science.[7]

I would have guessed, while waiting for Jin, my baby, my son, to arrive, that becoming a mother would be like becoming a wife, if not more so—a rebirth into a self created through relationship, a relationship so vast and so meaningful that it remakes your being. I don't mean it overwrites you or swallows you up. I mean your bond causes you both to lean so far in to one another that a core piece of you changes, as if you mutually recoded your DNA. I would not have put it like this at the time, but I had a deep and inchoate sense that this change would occur. I would not have guessed I would be remade, through motherhood, as a child too, that the presence of my son would make me a very different daughter.

Part III

AFTER

5.

Baby: And to My Name as Son

WHEN WAITING FOR Jin to come, I became obsessed with the whole concept of adoption. I read every article, no matter how silly, about celebrities who adopt, and I also read everything I could find about adoption in history. I could rattle off random facts about each one of Angelina Jolie's adopted children. I knew the name of Zahara's pediatrician—I interviewed her, in fact—and that her eldest son Maddox's nickname was Madness. I read Hammurabi's Code, the set of ancient Babylonian laws that form the first set of written laws of any type, and the first set of laws governing adoption. I read documents from the early American orphan trains, and nonfiction books like Stella Lanyard's *Aristocrats*, about the eighteenth-century Lennox sisters; fertile Emily gave childless Louisa one of her daughters to raise. The fact of adoption fascinated me and drew my attention; I stared to the point of intrusiveness at families with children of another race. I wanted to hear about every parent who had ever adopted, and imagined myself in Babylonia, eighteenth-century England, the early American West, or whatever time and place I happened to be reading about.

The laws of Hammurabi—he of the long, funky, rectangular beard, knotted as a chenille bedspread—were simple and meant to clarify the boundaries of family; his first law of adoption reads: "If a man adopt a child and to his name as son, and rear him, this grown son cannot be demanded back again." They are full of strange and compelling details: that the children of vestal virgins could be adopted without parental consent; that an infertile wife could choose a servant to bear a child for her by her husband, and the child would be legally and fully hers, but the servant could not then be dismissed.

I tried to imagine being this birth mother, chosen to bear a child only to have her child raised as another woman's, the babe right under her feet and perhaps partially in her care, though the law did not acknowledge her. Would this mother be socialized enough to accept the child as truly belonging to the woman their law called mother? Would the wife choose a lovely maidservant—wanting a child with pretty features—or worry about living with a beautiful woman whom her husband had slept with and who could never be banished from her home? It was an arrangement similar to our surrogacy, if the surrogate lived with you permanently but without personal freedom. Our surrogacy practices have led to court challenges by surrogate mothers who changed their minds; I expect the Babylonians faced their own challenges too. We know so little of what these families, similar to ours in many external ways, would have felt like. In reporting history, we tend to assume that the written codes of the group apply to everyone emotionally, as if a society can be other than a collection of individuals, each with his or her own way of relating to the world.

Would the birth mothers have nursed their babies, I wondered, and how would that feel to me if that had been my arrangement, an adoptive mom with this slip of a thing in my arms, all kicky legs and masses of dark hair? He cried a lot for those first few weeks after arrival. Agencies call it the transition time. Babies cry, partly, because you—your smell, your house, your food—are strange to them. In Jin's case, he had jet lag and wanted to sleep during the day and stay up all night. He had been fed in Korea with a bottle with a fast-flow nipple, but it took me several days to realize that; his face grew red when he drank from our bottles, and after getting down a couple of ounces of formula he screamed. We tried different bottles and different nipples but didn't think to try fast-flow nipples, the ones with large holes; pediatricians here frown on them. It took me ages to think of the simple solution of checking the bottle Jin had arrived with. Sure enough, the hole in the nipple looked like a large darning needle had made it. He had been working too hard, by his standards, for his food.

I remember standing in department stores in the infant section, wondering how there could be so many bottles and nipples, all claiming to be the closest to the real thing, when the human nipple comes, from a baby's viewpoint, in pretty much one variety.

The Romans, especially the wealthy patrician classes, adopted many of their children, including their heirs, and gave up their children to be adopted frequently too. Romans, particularly the upper classes, kept children in check, due to the expense. Daughters had to be dowered; sons had to be given something to inherit, and Romans did not believe in breaking up family lands to accommodate the needs of multiple boys. At birth, every Roman child was presented to its father, who decided whether to keep the child or abandon it. Keeping the child was no guarantee that the relationship would last forever; adult children got swapped around through adoption and relinquishment, sometimes, like marriage, as a way to cement ties between powerful families.[8]

It's hard to interpret what the Roman practice of child abandonment actually meant; the Latin word for exposure—*expositio*—translates as something like our English "exposition" and has more of a sense of display than death. The evidence we have from the Romans' many written records shows a death rate among abandoned children not too far above normal infant mortality, so many of these children must have been taken up by others, though often into slavery or prostitution. Roman cities commonly had a public area with columns called *lactaria* or "nursing" columns, so-called because parents abandoned nursing infants at their bases.[9]

Biological parents must in many cases have kept an eye on

their young, as parents of abandoned children—generally fathers, as Roman children belonged to their fathers for much of their lives—often sought to gain the children back, generally when the child had grown into an adult. Adopted children were often made heirs or taught a trade, and birth parents may have been trying to cash in by going to court for the child's return; they seem to have suffered no stigma for abandoning them. Roman law stipulated only that fathers who demanded their children back refund the cost of rearing them. Adoptive fathers could fight these requests, and did. One such father argued in court to block removal of the son he had raised:

> During the time that our son was away at war...whose was he? Was it not I who hung from the city walls in suspense? Not I who seized everyone returning from the battlefield? Not I who, desperate, fell upon the messengers? Who bandaged his wounds when he returned? Who washed away the blood?[10]

What moves me in this courtroom quote is the all-powerful Roman father's naked emotion, waiting on the walls of the city for any sign of his beloved child, performing the slave's job of dressing his child's wounds.

Foundlings occupied an ambiguous legal space in the household. They were generally raised as *alumni,* somewhat like our foster children. They could live as part of the family and even be made heirs, but as only a Roman father could legally relinquish a child, the birth father could reassert rights over a foundling. At the same time, while formal adoption often involved managing inheritance and death rituals, along with other family rituals, taking in an *alumnus* often had no motive beyond the desire to care for the child. The child's devotion to an adoptive parent was proverbial in ancient Rome; to be loved as if by an *alumnus* meant strong attachment.

❧

In my own early baby days, I had a lot in common with that Roman adoptive father. I wanted to do things for my baby—the more elaborate, the better. If Jin kept me up all night, as he did for the first few weeks, I resisted and yet relished the exhaustion. We took long baths together. I spent hours with my head canted to the side in the back seat of the car, or angled forward from the neck, leaning into his body in my lap, or in the crib, so that he could play with my hair. My neck ached all the time. If he fell asleep on my lap, I didn't move until he woke up. I wanted so much for the gods to understand that I deserved this child.

We nicknamed Jin "Woozlebug"—an old term for the Jersey Devil, a mythical winged and horse-faced creature that haunted my home state—or "Bug."

At times the enormous responsibility of a baby, the amount we didn't know, overwhelmed us. We panicked: I called my friend Rosina and had her rush over to check one of Jin's first diapers. The foul, greenish stuff in it did not seem as if it could have been produced by a healthy infant.

"It's a change in diet, that's all," she said, looking from the diaper I had carefully saved on one corner of the changing table to my face. "You're doing fine. You're doing a great job," she added kindly. Women would say that to me then. I clung to the assurances and didn't think about the fact that these women couldn't possibly know what kind of job I was doing, and that I must have exuded an awful lot of insecurity for them to bother to pretend they did.

Who could have imagined the enormous range of emotions then? I loved my baby, but was in the process of falling in love with him. At times—as when, before the fast-flow nipples, he sucked a quarter cup of formula then screamed in outrage—I looked at him, thinking, who are you?

Bruce stopped me on the stairs when Jin had been with us several weeks. "I realized I really love him now."

I said, "I know," though what we had felt before was not *not-*love. Both of us put our hearts into Jin, slept with him, lifted him giggling into the air, had his face in our minds as the last thing we saw before falling asleep and the image that rose in front of us as soon as we awoke. We would have begged for him from a witness chair in court, like that Roman father.

Three days after Jin's arrival Bruce leapt out of bed, still asleep and frantically jerking some invisible object from his back.

"He's in the pack! He's in the pack!" he urged the dark air. In a nightmare Bruce had had Jin in his backpack and had lain down on him; he jumped out of bed to pull him off. We worried so about this vulnerable baby.

I had loved Jin before arrival as an abstraction, a slip of paper with a blurred photo, a thought of something tiny and sweet to hold. Now he was present—so present—a little package of likes and dislikes and quirks, a baby who would cry to grab hold of my hair then giggle when he got it, a hater of outerwear, a being who breathed out a sweet-scented breath onto the ledge of my shoulder, who found the world riling or enormously funny. He loved to stare at lightbulbs and trucks, and when some construction began around the corner from our house, involving a cement truck with its ruminative turn and a scooper, we would take him for a walk and park his stroller there for a while so that he could enjoy the trucks going about their slow business.

The feeling of his breath, the beat of his heart rocking its one-two into the palm of my hand, redrew all that mattered to me.

Before Jin arrived, Bruce and I signed up for an infant CPR class, in the spirit of doing whatever constituted responsible parenting. A Native American of the Lummi tribe, a tough, kind police officer, taught the class.

"What is the first thing you look for when you go into your kids' room and they're asleep?" he asked rhetorically. "You look for the covers rising and falling. You make sure they're breathing." I remember thinking, huh? How paranoid would parents have to be to check on whether their child's still *alive*? Then a few months later, I found myself looking into Jin's crib, making sure the covers were rising and falling.

Jin confused us. He fascinated us, and came more and more into focus as a little human being, who would suck our thumbs to go to sleep, loved our singing and rocking, lit up at the sight of our carefully prepared food but spat out the blueberries I picked.

His personality rose, day by day, to the surface, like someone slowly rising out of deep water. I made him smoked salmon in cream cheese, soft-cooked rice with milk, pureed vegetables. Bruce made crepes. Jin ate with a delirious smile on his face if he liked what he was eating, throwing food all over; our two dogs always circled his high chair while we chanted the theme from *Jaws*.

Jin pulled little bits of fuzz off his baby blankets and stuck it under his nose—above the thumb he sucked—to help him sleep. When he began to use words, both his favorite blanket and the bits it produced got named Fuzzy, and he screamed the word when he wanted to sleep: "Fuzzy! Fuzzy!" I learned to crazy-quilt, and made him a baby blanket out of bits of fabric with patterns reflecting all of his favorite things—lightbulbs, trucks, trains, dinosaurs, Band-Aids—with a pocket to hold extra fuzzy bits, which I plucked myself.

My baby and I always touched; when the three of us made the two-hour drive to Seattle to catch a plane or, later, to go to a children's show or museum, I'd have to keep my arm hanging into the backseat so Jin could clutch my hand, until my arm went dead, heavy, just a tool hanging from my shoulder. To love a baby as an abstraction is to love what babies have that's adorable: soft skin; toothless, ingratiating, and roguish smiles; needs we can understand and, normally, satisfy. You love the contract they represent with the future; they are something you have touched that will outlive you. To love a real, particular baby is to grasp their personalities more and more each day, to see how admirably these tiny, helpless beings cope with constructing a world that makes them happy. How they tell you what they want, with the tired cry, the just-waking-up cry, the hungry cry.

Jin would blink back at me in my "who are you" wonder, thinking, I imagine, some baby version of the same thought. I expect that can happen with birth children, but parents have a sense of those children's preexistence: their kicks, their swan dives under the skin. My child had lived in a world that didn't include me—that included all manner of trivial things, like yogurt and sponge cake, but not his mother. He had a world that was his and one that he had controlled to some degree, in the mute and refusing manner of babies; he hated blueberries, loved tofu, knew when he wanted to sleep and when he didn't. Some other woman—one I would not meet for many years— knew these things before me. Jin had slept to the shooing, cooing sounds of his native Korean.

It was November, with the Northwest's onslaughts of rain and storm-force winds, and Jin hated being zipped into his coat, just as he hated diaper changes, though in any other regard he loved touch. We had brought him to a place where this water-proof plush of coat was necessary and he flailed his limbs at us in protest. He had an astonishingly loud laugh, a deep rumble from down in the belly, which could turn into an equally loud wail.

"Some lungs on the wee bairn," a colleague of ours used to say. I looked to the sparse documents we had on Jin's birth parents to see if I could grasp any correlation. Did his calm stare reflect his studious birth father? Did his screams show a trace of his tattooed and free-spirited birth mother? What had become of his birth father's so-called exotic features? Jin, classically beautiful, could not be called exotic in the context of Korea; he wore the map of the country in his face, as my mother used to say of people stamped with their ethnicity.

I mused about these questions to my friend Lynne, who is herself a Korean adoptee—relinquished by her birth mother at the age of ten—and also an adoptive mother of three Korean-born children.

"Those reports are a bunch of bunk," she told me in her crisp way. "They have a stack of generic bios at the orphanages, they just randomly hand them out."

I never looked into the truth behind this comment; I suppose I never wanted to, though it wormed its way into my consciousness. Perhaps I knew nothing about my son. I imagined myself as that Roman father or mother, walking away from the *lactaria* with my new child. Unlike me, that parent would not have spent months filling out forms or talking to professionals, as I had, to be vetted for parenthood. He or she would have wondered, as I did, who this child was, and what bond would develop, and whether the child would drink the milk of a cow or a goat, or share the Roman enthusiasm for tiny delicacies, snails and oysters and dormice.

___

Many children in this world are not, and have never been, raised by their biological parents. Most young children are no longer raised by both in one household. For the past few years, births to single moms have risen to 40 percent of all births. Many kids are raised by neither biological parent but without a formal adoption decree passing them off to someone else. This is true in my and my husband's families, and, as I asked around, I found that almost everyone has some story of a family member being moved around without formal adoption. Families have always been fluid—much more so than the type of fixed nuclear family we now think of as the norm—and parenting has always been both desirable and hard, in equal measure.

My student Trina told me the story of her grandmother, raised by an aunt and uncle: "My great-great-aunt was diagnosed with melancholia and her doctor recommended she obtain a baby... first she tried my great-uncle Fred, but he was a fussy baby and apparently too hard to handle, so the aunt and her husband gave him back and took my grandmother, who was a year or two older, instead. She lived with her aunt and uncle until she was married, only visiting her parents and brothers and sisters on occasion. She always knew she'd been given to her aunt and uncle and always referred to them as Uncle Fred and Aunt Flo."

My grandfather and my husband's father both got passed around throughout their childhoods. People of the Caribbean islands practice kinship fostering, and farm kids out, far more than Americans do, or ever have; even by Caribbean standards, though, my grandfather had a lot of homes. My grandfather's younger brother died of pneumonia aggravated by his mother's, my great-grandmother's, neglect. My grandfather was a melancholy man, and I imagine a melancholy boy. As long as I knew him he would sit up nights, hour by slow hour, doing nothing in the darkness.

At one point my grandfather lived as a kind of ward with two sea captains named Archer and Pilcher, I assume in Barbados. Wardship was a system of guardianship practiced in England, especially before adoption became legal there in the first half of the twentieth century. My grandfather's longest stay with anyone came when his mother left him with family friends named the Goslings. I met the Goslings when I was little, a couple who struck me as more ancient than anyone could be, dust caught in their wrinkles almost, like characters from myth. I never heard my grandfather mention his parents, but he talked about the Goslings all his life, as did my grandmother, with affection. I gathered they were the closest thing he ever had to what we would call parents.

My husband's father, Harold, was born in a tiny town in Georgia called Glenville, a string of trailer homes and every sixth one a church, or that's how it felt the times I visited. His mother, Sarah, my husband's grandmother, had strange aspirations: she had run a tearoom—a little lunchroom—in Atlanta; her son claimed she'd wanted to be an opera singer. Her husband was an alcoholic whom she married, divorced, and remarried, three times in total. I met Sarah just once, an old lady from a small Southern place who seemed geologic eons away from opera and ambition. She was remarkably bodily, in a way that hits certain old Southern ladies almost like a form of senescence. A heavy cane tap announced her arrival in the room, with her small, neat head of white hair and twisty country accent delivering a screed about her leaking gall bladder and arthritis that she declared, like some Flannery O'Connor character, had "done et through the bone."

After one of her divorces Sarah gave Harold away, keeping his younger brother, Joe. No one is entirely sure why. She needed to support herself. She was, Joe said, ambitious. But why she kept one and not the other we don't know. She does not seem to have given Joe a whole lot of attention. Perhaps he needed to believe she was an opera singer, an upwardly mobile tearoom mogul. Joe became a well-known doctor and Harold a lawyer with a night-school degree who worked at a low-wage job, removing people from their property for the government. He declared bankruptcy every seven years; all his kids endured a childhood of their father hollering for them to answer the phone and stall creditors. Both brothers became alcoholics.

One of Harold's sons married a woman whose mother was adopted, abandoned during the Great Depression. I don't know what conversations her adoptive parents had about her appearance on their doorstep, but they were thrilled to have her. She was a healthy newborn, wrapped in blankets, obviously left there after a lot of thought on the part of her birth mother. Her adoptive parents were well off; probably they had been selected for that, and for their lack of children. Caroline became a schoolteacher: I knew her for thirty years and heard her tell the basket story over and over again, always egged on by her husband, who loved it. She told it matter-of-factly, in the same tone she would have used to give the secret of her baked chicken (Coca-Cola).

Between 1910 and 1925, adoption dropped off in the US, due to a sudden social preoccupation with eugenics; the language of "bad blood," "enfeebled parents," and "congenital bent to criminality" littered public discussion of abandoned and poor children (and echoes the occasional "bad genes" language of our own time). Adoption rose dramatically after the Second World War, when a new population of war orphans sprang up domestically and abroad, and the science of eugenics lay in disgrace on the floor of Josef Mengele's lab.

Child abandonment is still a problem in the US, with many states responding to the problem of abandoned newborns by creating safe sites where young mothers can drop off newborns who might otherwise be left in danger. One such law, Nebraska's, backfired; it designated infant haven areas at hospitals but failed to include an age limit. When the law was enacted, thirty-five older children, ranging in age from ten to seventeen, were left at Nebraska hospitals by mothers who claimed the children had become defiant and unmanageable; in some cases, the parents could not afford the psychiatric care their children needed. Many parents had driven to Nebraska from other states. The Nebraska legislature quickly convened and limited the age of safe-haven children to one month.

In Europe, child abandonment was widespread well into the nineteenth century. In the eighteenth century, between 10 and 40 percent of all children in urban areas were abandoned. While poverty accounts for much child abandonment, it is not always the rule; in some societies, such as ancient Rome, wealthy parents were actually more inclined than poor ones to give up their children.

The eighteenth-century French philosopher Jean-Jacques Rousseau, whose writings influenced this country's Founding Fathers and seeded the thinking of our revolution, abandoned all five of his children to a foundling hospital. In his *Confessions*, he gave his reasons: he did not feel he could be both a father and a writer, and he considered their mother, a seamstress named Thérèse, too "ill brought up" to raise them properly. For many years he considered his decision to be "so good, so sensible" that he did not question it, though eventually he regretted it and searched for his eldest son. Rousseau's own behavior belied his advice to mothers—very high-nurture for the period—whom he advised to breast-feed their infants themselves.

As far as we can tell from historical records, the rate of child deaths has never matched the rate of abandonment. As there have always been parents who could not meet the needs of their children, there have always been others eager to parent.

Proof of the frequency of child abandonment and child rescue lies in ongoing cultural fears of the abandoned child, an image that has haunted cultures in the West since antiquity, with the dangers of a casual encounter with an unrecognized adult child a running theme in behavioral codes and literature from classical societies through the Middle Ages and beyond. The Oedipus story illustrates the incest danger in having abandoned children out in the world, unknown to their biological parents; Oedipus not only had sex with his mother, he killed his father. Classical moralists as well as—more surprisingly—early church fathers like Justin Martyr and Clement of Alexandria warned men against going to brothels on the grounds that they might unknowingly have sex with their own daughter, or possibly a sister.[11]

Though children have been given up by parents throughout the ages, it's worth remembering that at least the potential for great love between parents and children has always existed too. Adoption historians point out that the greatest increase in abandonment in Europe happened during the period when Western Europeans began to consider childhood as a separate— and sentimentalized—state of life.

Historically, children were considered as if they were small adults—capable of the same work, and having the same emotional and physical needs, as the people who made them, a philosophy that arose from lives committed to agriculture and wide patterns of extended relationships. The concept of a separate state of being called childhood—with its own emotional demands and ways of thinking about the world—only arose in the last two centuries in the West, driven by the rise of the concept of the nuclear family and the idealization of the smaller family unit. No amount of romanticization of the family and childhood, though, changed the rate at which parents opted out, for one reason or another, of parenthood.

⟶

Several aspects of my adoption would puzzle those folks of the ancient world, for whom choosing a birth mother from among your slaves, or bending down at a marble column in a public square to pick out a baby, would seem normal. It would have seemed strange then that my husband and I had to prove ourselves worthy of this child, that the child's good was placed at the center of the process of taking him in, with a legal procedure for determining the fitness of would-be parents. Transracial adoption is also historically unusual, though intertribal adoption occurs throughout Oceania and transracial adoption has certainly taken place. (President Andrew Jackson, the famous Indian fighter, adopted a Creek baby he named Lyncoya and intended to send to West Point, though the child died young.) Adoptive parents have generally stayed within their own ethnic, racial, or clan groups, even within loose networks of extended family and close friends.

Those Romans or Babylonians or Lennox sisters would look at my infant's eyes and skin tone and straight black hair, being held in the arms of one who looks classically southern Mediterranean, with wonder.

Some cultures developed rituals to permit adoption from outside the social group. I found, reading the *Journal of the Royal Anthropological Society*, the story of adoption among the Man cultural group of Hong Kong.[12] Among the Man, an adoptive father who ventured outside his clan had to give a lavish banquet at which guests could ask him to loan them any sum of money they wished without repayment, mocked his inability to produce children and complained about the miserable quality of the food, all in order to get his son accepted into the clan lineage. (I told this to my friend Xu Xi, a native of Hong Kong, who laughed and said, "That's incredibly Chinese! Get the insults out of the way so you can get on with things.") The classical Chinese adopted foundlings, but these children generally could not inherit.

Nurture can be one of life's great pleasures, if the time, the resources, and the desire are in place. There are always people who want children; there are always people who can't handle them, or not for long. My own father, born into poverty with a sick mother, was given to another woman to nurse. The wealthy have nannies and housekeepers and tutors, but in the past—and this is still true in many countries—servants earned so little that even lower-income families might have a few. Poor families needed everyone possible to be working; children might receive rough nurture from an older sibling or cousin for a few years, and begin an adult routine of field or factory work before age ten.

The working poor of the world—which was all of them, before social safety nets came to give some relief in industrialized countries—often dealt with young children by restraining them, maybe swaddling them or cooping them up somehow at the edge of a field while the parents labored on the farm. I remember seeing, in a museum, a painting of a child restrained in a device that looked like a butter churn, except that where the paddle would normally be, a doleful toddler's head poked out.

Children cost more than we expect, may be more defiant or less affectionate than pleases us. Or they enter our lives somehow and become necessary to us, more loving, more smart or lovable than we could have imagined, and we crave their presence. We know from court testimony, wills, epitaphs, and the wording of laws that human beings have always been capable of deeply loving children, hanging over the walls of the city just to see the beloved face return from war.

～

In England, legal adoption did not exist until 1926. From the start, though the US borrowed much of England's legal system, it differed in the area of adoption law. We have always been a restless people, with fluid families and at our core a rejection of England's ritualized faith in bloodlines. And we've always had many forms of apprenticeships and fostering. Orphanages existed here by 1800, and orphanage managers placed children in homes through adoption, though there was often little or no scrutiny of how children were treated after placement.

Not until 1851, in Massachusetts, did a provision wend its way into law declaring that adoption should be first and foremost "for the good of the child," and that it would be the job of a qualified judge to determine whether adoptive parents were "fit and proper." The law also stated that adopted children were to have the same rights "as if the child had been born in lawful wedlock." The change in an adoptive child's legal status, so simply phrased, was enormous. Until that time, even children who were adopted—and there were a great number, some placed by early adoption crusaders who took it on themselves to scrutinize the adoptive home on behalf of their charges—had to be placed in the home as "indentures," a contract relationship that implies an exchange of labor. Children could be loved, or they could become glorified servants or field hands. Gradually, after the Massachusetts law passed, the rest of the country passed similar legislation.

Many American orphanages in the early days were unpleasant, unsanitary, and lacked proper food. Abandoned children were placed with criminals, or with those who were incarcerated for mental illness. In the early nineteenth century, urban areas teemed with more human beings per square mile than any place on earth, many of them homeless children. Charles Loring Brace founded New York's Children's Aid Society in 1853—after the Massachusetts legislation passed, introducing the concept of the good of the child as a factor in placement—and for forty years placed city children in homes out West, delivering them on so-called "orphan trains."

He believed that country air and a farmer's work ethic would deliver children from the depravity created by slums and orphanages in the cities. Eighty-four thousand children eventually traveled on these trains. Unfortunately, Brace also believed that his charges should be brought up in Protestant homes, and he sometimes removed children from intact homes with poorer Catholic or Jewish parents.

Even without that enormous blemish on his record, we would not recognize Brace as a champion of children. Orphan trains ran for seventy-odd years; at each stop, the children were yanked from the train to stand on the platform for inspection by farm families. Desirable children—many of whom would not be adopted legally, but simply became field hands—were older, healthy, and strong. Some of the orphan train children were welcomed into the family and loved, but there's plenty of evidence that many were not.

Fortunately, there were orphanages with remarkable success in placing children, including infants, for adoption in loving homes, thanks to some remarkable people in the early child welfare movement. Two sisters, Anstrice and Eunice Fellowes, campaigned through their newsletter *Orphans' Advocate* for changes in the law to give equality in the family to adopted children, and urged Massachusetts to pass its landmark adoption law of 1851. The unmarried sisters also ran an adoption agency that placed children with families for free, provided the children would be treated "as equal members of the family circle." In the early days of American adoption, parents rarely adopted babies; infants' needs, and inability to contribute to the home, made them unlikely candidates, except through the efforts of advocates like the Fellowes sisters.

I imagine myself in the eyes of a farmer who has poked and prodded his soon-to-be son on a train platform, a sturdy boy, possibly Semitic or Italian but with familiar enough features—not a child of another race. The farmer, who grows corn and apples and raises animals for meat, sees me. I wait at an echoing airport for the infant I've never set eyes on—who is four months older than the only photo I have, and therefore almost completely unfamiliar—at a place where not trains but planes deliver infants. I'm sobbing over that infant, first afraid to hold him, then clinging to him as if he were a branch in the ocean. Maybe in that farmer's poking and prodding of the boy, an unexpected choke of sentiment forms in his throat. Maybe we're not so different.

⌒

Overseas adoption, which began at the end of the Second World War, started as a way to place children orphaned by the war, mostly Caucasian children from Germany and Greece, in homes far removed from years of fighting. Japanese children also were placed overseas, and the influx of children left homeless by war opened the door to transracial adoption. During the Korean War, international adoption became more and more often transracial, although racial sorting among babies, reflecting the attitudes of society at large, continued; Holt, the leading international adoption agency, which was founded by an American soldier during the Korean War, would place Asian infants with white parents, but placed Afro-Asian babies (the children of GIs) with African American parents.

When Jin first came to us, a woman approached us in a diner to tell us his "slanty eyes were so cute." Random people told us he would be skilled at math and good at using computers because "they are." I developed a practiced glare for these comments. We might have been better off with a transition ritual like the Man people of China: one large meal in which everyone could get their stupid remarks out of the way.

At home I held Jin in my arms, carried him all day or wore him in a front-pack, let him sleep on my lap. I studied his hair and his face. Those wild tufts of hair that began in the middle of his head, close to the fontanelle. Thick straight hair as long as my fingers, crescent eyes light-lidded, those dimples. Jin, unlike my husband and me, even as a baby had visible muscles: little deltoids on top of his shoulders, biceps that stood out under his baby fat. As I fell more and more in love with him the wonder of *not-me* lit the way: the eyes that came so distinctly from someone else, the muscles he inherited from a set of genes that had also built the frame of a body very different from Bruce's and mine.

How would it have been to respond honestly to those statements I hated: yes, these eyes are different from yours, and mine. Yes, he will be good at things that are foreign to me. And that is why I love him so much. For his otherness, his discontinuity with my flesh. I would have loved the babies I'd been pregnant with, had I had them, and I imagine part of that love would be seeing those miraculous resurrections wrought by genetics: a dead parent's smile, a loved spouse's eyes. We build as strong a love on a deep and abiding tenderness and awe at what we don't ourselves possess, what we haven't had in our lives before, even in the form of other family members. This could be my closing speech at my adoption banquet.

It is a beautiful part of adoption that we create a love based, partially, on difference: my son's thick heavy hair, skin a darker olive than my yellowy southern Mediterranean cast. His astonishing spatial sense: at two and a half, he used to give me driving directions, barking them out from his car seat. As he grows, I see him become at once more like me, more Korean, and more himself. In the same way that the Roman father who could not claim the Roman prerogative of blood cried out, "Whose was he? Was it not I who hung from the city walls in suspense?" about a young man whose eyes and hair and fingers bore the blueprint of someone else, and who had grown fully into his difference, still leaving a father pining for him on the walls of the city.

6.

One Year Old:
Separation Anxieties

A T OUR PARTY for our friend Pam, we felt blessed, in love
with one another and with our new son, outside of time.
We'd learn that in this game of parenting, these moments are
temporary breathers. In a few years Clare, the sweet doctor at
our party, would lose her two daughters, Blake and Cori, in the
Alaska Airlines flight that crashed off the coast of California en
route from Puerto Vallarta, Mexico, in 2000.

We did not know Clare well. She was a friend of Pam's. The
death of her children, and of several other children in our neighborhood orbit, made my own child's fragility achingly close. I
traveled occasionally for work, but I hated traveling then, and I
could work myself into a sweaty panic just sitting in my university office away from home; my child's safety felt dependent on
a secret formula: distance from my body = danger. Jin walked
early—he took his first full steps at ten months—giving him a
lot of mobility coupled with his strong will. At a little over a year
old, he climbed out of his crib, landing on the floor with an awful

thunk. We raced up the stairs to find him giggling in the middle of his bedroom floor. If something caught his eye, he might dart away from me into whatever dangers, such as traffic, happened to be between him and the thing he wanted.

My father is the kind of parent who's perpetually worried, who calls to make sure the plane didn't crash, who once called our house over and over again and hung up, too choked by sobs to speak, because, it turned out, I had called him and said, "Oh, I called you by accident," and he thought he heard, "I had an accident."

I discovered new and unparalleled similarities between my father and me.

In the US today, adoption is not legally granted until the child has been in your home for a six-month probationary period. Until that visit to the courtroom, we—and I expect most adoptive parents—imagined scenarios in which the adoption could be denied. Jin might hurt himself, have an accident or become sick, in a way that might make us seem negligent. I could feel the terror of losing him without even a plausible event to attach to it. It is a strange feeling, to live so utterly immersed in being a mother—caring for my child, carrying him all day, making his food while he sleeps—while knowing at the same time that legally you're not a mother, quite.

Jin loved for us to swing him up in the air by the arms as we walked down the street. One day we were doing this and he fell to the ground screaming. And kept screaming, clutching at his elbow.

"We have to get him to the doctor," said Bruce

"We can't! What will they think? What if they think we hurt him on purpose?" I felt a heart-thumping panic, but we rushed him to the doctor. He was clearly in pain, and couldn't stop crying.

I was in tears at the doctor's office, when a no-nonsense nurse pulled Jin into an exam room and shoved his elbow joint back into place with a swift yank.

"Nursemaid's elbow, they all get it," she said shortly. "Kids love to be swung, but their joints are soft." She did not even bother consulting with the doctor. My knees went weak. Of course. Kids love to be swung. Nursemaid's elbow, they all get it.

At a year and a half, Jin developed separation anxiety—normal at that age, though his grew extreme. He howled when I left the room. If we hired a babysitter, Bruce would meet her and I would sneak out and wait around the corner; if I departed the house in front of Jin he'd be inconsolable. Once I went to the restroom in an Old Spaghetti Factory restaurant, a cavernous family place, and Jin screamed, wriggled out of his booster seat somehow, and ran in a panic after me, crashing into the ladies' room and diving under the door of my stall. This separation anxiety made life harder for a while, but I admired the kid's spirit.

And, I had to admit, I took his point. Of course you don't know if someone who's left the room will ever come back. They often don't, in this life. Children don't practice magical or pretend thinking; we adults do, and perhaps that's why at times babies and toddlers seem so prescient.

The day came finally when we went before the judge in his chambers, with a lawyer we had spoken to maybe twice, and became Jin's parents in the eyes of the state. Jin took our names, along with the one he had arrived with and that we loved: it was all him. It took place at 7 a.m., far too early for us and our little night owl. We had to spend many minutes just getting him to wake up, and his thick hair stuck straight up, defying our spit-slicking. We dressed him and ourselves in the best clothes we could find. Bruce wore a jacket and tie and I wore a blue dress, not fancy, but the best I had in those first post-grad-school job days. Jin wore a rather stiff white shirt and dark pants, under his tired, cranky face.

The thin, distracted judge asked us Jin's new name, and when Bruce said, "Jin Woo Raphael," he gave us an arch little grin. The Raphael came from my side, a traditional male name in my father's Italian family. Jin's surname, the same as my husband's, is very, very Southern.

The two women friends who came with us and served as witnesses said later that they'd expected me to cry. I had no urge to cry. I just felt a tremendous relief, knowing that any ordinary accident could not undo this tie between me and my son.

Even after the adoption was finalized, Jin did not become an American citizen. That took place a few months later. If we adopted Jin now, this would not be the case: new legislation creates citizens out of children at the time of adoption. Back then, we had to take him to do what any would-be citizen had to do: go to the Naturalization Office and be sworn in. We applied for a time and got a terse form scheduling us for 8 a.m. I wrote back and pointed out that we had a two-hour drive to the INS office in Seattle, and in return we got another terse form rescheduling us for 7:30 a.m.

We joined a group of Sikhs, Somalis, Chinese, Thais, snaking in a long line out of the grimy immigration office on the edge of the International District, all of them looking very patient, which we were not. When we finally got inside, we waited and waited for Jin's name to be called. Jin drooled on his onesie as the immigration official asked him quite seriously if he would pledge to bear arms for the United States. We said yes for him, unsure whether or not to hold his chubby arm up in the air.

I wonder now that, with all the worrying I did about Jin— and the hard lesson of just how vulnerable our children can be—I did not worry at this moment but felt a wash of calm. Jin the US citizen could drive to Canada with us. And Jin the US citizen could not be deported, unlikely as deportation would be. I suppose imagining this happy and fleshy little child in a soldier's camouflage, toting a gun, was too ludicrous, too far in the future to seem real. I thought of my great-grandparents on my father's side, and my grandparents on my mother's, all immigrants, swearing to protect the flag. In this moment Jin, their nonbiological offspring, resembled them more than perhaps any other of their descendants did. For them, adults, the promise to bear arms was theoretical. For Jin, a child, it could come to pass.

Not too long after Jin's swearing-in as an American citizen, we celebrated his first birthday. If I ask Jin about this party, the largest we've thrown him to date, he says he remembers it, but I think he remembers us telling him about it over and over again. We threw him a traditional Korean *tol*, a first birthday party, one of the most important birthday celebrations in Korea (another is the sixtieth). Jin wore a scratchy colorful *hanbok*, a traditional

Korean outfit with loose pants and a cone-shaped hat covered with Chinese characters, and we held a ceremony where he sat at a small table loaded with symbolic objects brought by all the guests and reached for the things that would define the course of his life—a scholar's brush and a cooking spoon, as it turned out.

For Jin's second birthday, which he does seem to remember, I made him a birthday cake consisting of many small cakes decorated as a train. Each "car" carried its own cargo, a candy fantasy with sugar bricks and licorice snipped to look like logs. The cars had nonpareil wheels and rode on a green-tinted fondant ground with licorice-whip tracks and green coconut grass.

This cake was one of many I used to make him, sometimes entirely odd and whimsical. It has to do with young children; you are always with them. You have in front of you this child that you love. If you think for a second about how much you love this child, the bonding hormone oxytocin will swish through your body like blood or lymph. And you have his world more or less under your own order and you have the option of filling it with beauty, or mystery, with trains that run on licorice whips through coconut. I imagined him staring at my cake and pulling pieces off it to eat, little by little—a speckled candy rock, a licorice log. Instead, he stared pensively but only for a second, and picked up as much of the thing as he could and stuffed it into his mouth.

I cannot save him from those bad things that happen—out of the clear blue sky, like a plane falling—whether they are accidents or wars starting up. I could bake up fantasies that promised to take him away to worlds I created, of sweet and sugar.

Part IV

GROWING UP

7.

Ages Two and Three:
The Doctor of Siena

J IN'S TERRIBLE TWOS hit at age two and a half exactly, with
the suddenness of some transformation from myth. The full
moon came out, the gods were jealous, some spell turned our
little icon of Zen into, at times, a snarling werewolf.

I, with my twenty-odd mostly younger cousins, at least knew
what a tantruming child looked like. Bruce, the youngest of five
and with no other children in his extended family, didn't have
that luxury. So one day, he ran outside yelling, "Jin's having a
seizure!"

I ran into the house and looked at Jin, thrashing around
red-faced on the floor.

"Noooooo," he shrieked, throwing himself around and around
like a prone dervish. "NOOOOOOOOOONOOOOOOOOOO,"
and something that sounded like "vik-ooom."

"What happened?"

"He was playing with the vacuum cleaner and I took it away."

"Bruce. That's a *tantrum*." Jin adored vacuum cleaners. I

imagine Bruce took it away because Jin was due for a nap, which meant Jin was tired as well as frustrated. He lay on his back on the floor, kicking and yelling for a good five minutes until he wore himself out and allowed himself to be carried, limp, to his crib.

Throughout Jin's young childhood, Bruce had a penchant for histrionic diagnoses. He would come and get me in a panic, saying that there appeared to be a dying bird trapped in Jin's room but he couldn't find it—the "bird" turned out to be Jin's croup cough, a fact Bruce discovered when he carried our toddler down the stairs and the dying bird sounds, caw-y and startling, came out of our toddler's innocuous and pudgy little self. ("I make silly sound noises," Jin said by way of explanation.) An ear infection became "nocturnal seizure disorder," an ailment Bruce pulled from the *Merck Medical Manual*, and he argued with the doctor at the emergency room. We both diagnosed Jin with blood in his urine and went through nurse after nurse on the pediatric hotline before noticing that we had the same strikingly crimson pee and we'd all eaten beets for lunch.

Jin had a year of tantrums, several times a week, yelling, kicking, and pounding affairs that threatened the lives of our old fir floors. He had night terrors too, something most children experience, but a scary thing to witness: he would leap up in bed shrieking terribly, eyes open, though he could not be fully wakened or see or hear me as I tried to comfort him. I held Jin in my arms once a week or so as he stared into my eyes screaming "Mommy! Mommy!" and I could see in his blind, frantic pupils that in the world he was in, his mommy inexplicably would not come. It took ten or fifteen minutes to get through an episode, which often happened without Jin ever waking up; he would finally just go limp in my arms, still asleep, but at peace.

When Jin was just three, we all flew to Siena, Italy. Bruce and I took eleven writing students for the month of August. As it happened, the fiction writer we planned to go with couldn't go, and since we offered a term's worth of credit in a month, each class met for two hours a day. I took over the fiction class along with the nonfiction class I was scheduled for, and taught for four hours a day in a severe Tuscan heat wave. We had no air-conditioning, and between teaching and seeing students after class, I went from being a mom who had been available a great deal of the time—on maternity leave, then sabbatical the first few years of Jin's life, and even when I taught, I taught half-time—to the Great Disappearing Sweaty and Crabby Mother.

Jin was too hot; he was, though we didn't know it yet, slightly sick, as he always was then; his mom had no time for him anymore, and everywhere we went he wanted something: gelato, toys from the toy store across the street, candy. I was overwhelmed with love and with confusion at Jin's toddler negativism, which accelerated in this strange, hot, new place. Pretty much everything we tried to do elicited that toddler's "No!," a pulling away at the arm. Jin bolted into stores and begged candy, ran from us, even smacked me a few times. When he didn't get his way he threw himself down and screamed. The Sienese should have taught me a lesson: they found tantrums adorable, huddling around to watch, murmuring "*spiritoso*" (spirited), "*carino*" (darling).

Jin was not being an easy child. I, on the other hand, was not being an easy parent. I had made myself far too busy, after being at Jin's disposal for much of his life. I didn't think about these things, or not much. I thought, to be honest, about adoption. I spiraled down into all the warnings I had ever received about adopted children from family, from misinformed people I barely knew, instead of thinking: at three kids get tantrummy. And I'm not around enough. I'm stressed with too much student work. Which he's very much not used to.

Instead I thought: he has the adopted child's primal wound, a concept I had read about in the book of the same name, a book arguing that adopted children feel innate loss and damage no matter what adoptive parents bring to them.

He's not really bonded to me, I thought. Things are going wrong, wrong. I felt panicked in the pit of my stomach.

I made Jin what he and I called cold towels, towels wrung out in cold water, laid over him to cool him down enough to sleep. We let him splash around in our apartment's deep sink. A pigeon family laid eggs on the window ledge across from ours— which Jin could see from his sink-tub—and the month grew into a lesson in being mother and child: as the chicks hatched, yowly beaked fluff growing from helplessness to flying. I tried to meet with my students and keep up with their stories and essays, sweating and mopping myself in what was, even for Italy in August, phenomenally hot weather, over one hundred degrees for more than a week.

The program housed us in an apartment down the street from the medieval cathedral of San Domenico, the family church of St. Catherine of Siena. Catherine, who came from a family of twenty-six, cut off her hair to become ugly to potential husbands and joined an order of lay sisters. She traveled to Avignon and scolded the pope into returning to Rome, and brokered peace agreements between city-states. She is one of two Italian saints considered doctors of the church in Italy, an illiterate woman who claimed that Jesus taught her to write, and who became one of the Italian language's great stylists. I have always loved Catherine. San Domenico houses a portrait of her done from life, in a nun's robes, holding a lily; she droops in her wimple, the flower droops. The cathedral also holds her finger and head.

Finally, my resources depleted, I walked down our cobblestone street in some spare moment and knelt before Catherine's statue. Please, Catherine, I prayed to this saint who had been determined never to marry and bear children, make me a mother. I admired the sacred head, the grim humor of her jaw with just a stretch, like old tape, of skin. This seems weird to me now, though I am a Catholic. Prayer to solve problems has never made any sense to me; yes, I understand an attitude of meditation, of expectant connection, but asking for things? That seems like tipping the cosmic balance in some unfair way, though I've followed my aunt Philomena through Italy, lighting votive candles with her as she told me that each new church you entered granted you a special wish.

I was confused and afraid—of what I had done as a mother, and what I had failed to do—and out of ideas, so I went to St. Catherine and said some equivalent of, Look, if you're there, and your body sure has shown some staying power, please help me out here. Make me as profoundly good a mother as I want so very, very much to be.

That is an unanswerable prayer, but one that matters

in the stakes you've thrown down. Just that saying, Please, I so want not to fuck this up, please let just anything else be fucked up in my life but not this.

Jin became friends with a priest during that stay in Siena, a very young, thin man with a scholarly face who spoke a slow and quiet, highly accented English. He lived at San Domenico and we ran into him almost every day, and while I always greeted the priest, whose name I can't recall, it would be he and Jin who stopped and talked. Jin used to walk up to the young father and ask him questions. Jin did that as soon as he had language, until he became a self-conscious teenager; he'd walk up to people and question them, politely and with real curiosity, about whatever he might want to know: what movies they watched if he saw them in a video store, if they had children.

I don't remember how Jin and this priest's friendship started, but I do remember one day when they were talking and Jin asked, "Why can't I see God?"

"Because," the priest replied in his slow and calm and consonantal English, "He is too near." Then he added, "He is nearer to you than you are to yourself."

I would like to say that answer satisfied Jin in some way, but it did not. It seemed very beautiful to me, but the logic of it eluded a three-year-old.

⌒

Within a few months of arriving back home, Jin was diagnosed with asthma. He went through a year of antibiotics for his constant respiratory infections, which had made him so exhausted and cranky. His temper expanded and contracted with his airways. By the time we finally had his adenoids removed—they had become a vector of infection—he mellowed into a much calmer kid.

"Walking pneumonia?" Bruce said when I called him from the doctor's one day with the usual diagnosis. "They should call it tantruming pneumonia."

Perhaps I don't give Catherine, the great doctor of the spirit, enough credit, and those earthly doctors, who treated Jin's asthma rather than my soul, too much. She may have intervened. Perhaps prayer—at least the kind you put everything you have into, and let it all be at stake—can work. Perhaps I have Catherine to thank that Jin and I still talk about his day in the car when I pick him up from school, and put our heads together and discuss how much we loved the Curtain Call firework on this Fourth of July. Or the Catherine Wheel, though the flaming Catherine who gives her name to this burst of light is a different one.

When I think back on raising a child, I picture a long process of losing control. You have some control with a baby, unless that baby has a serious illness; you can walk him or her around the house through pretty much any earache or sore gums—something that would be lovely to do with a teenager, but by adolescence contact comfort no longer cures many ills, and it would be, in my son's case at least, like hoisting a small giraffe. We could bring our baby bits of fuzzy and make him happy—or, at least, less upset.

I used to sing Jin to sleep, and as I didn't know many actual lullabies, I sang folk songs. They were gloomy and violent, as folk songs often are; Jin's favorite was the long, dismal song in which Lord Randall tells his mother he has been fed "eels and strong poison" by his lover and is dying. "What happened to your two dogs?" asks the mother, and Lord Randall says, "Oh, they cried and they died there," meaning, at the lover's house. I sang and sang to Jin in Italy, in the insomniac heat. I sang my throat sore and then hummed. I remember thinking, When Jin understands this song, that will be a fall from innocence, in the same way that seeing your child learn to lie or to use words to hurt you, something toddlers pick up, is a fall from innocence. I felt about that development the way Bruce had felt about high chairs. Let the child stay soothed by words, whatever those words are, I might have put it. Don't let him discover how even a story can hurt.

One night in Siena, Jin raised his head out of the half-coma sleep that young children sleep and said, "Why they cry and they die there, Mama? Why?" And I said, "Go back to sleep, I'll sing something else," and I did.

8.

Early Childhood:
Of Many Born

W E USED TO watch the video of Jin's arrival every year on November 21, his arrival day. I had made him an arrival scrapbook to look at in the future, with the first photo we had of him and pictures of us waiting for him at the airport, then holding him, changing his first diaper, riding home with him to Bellingham. Around the age of seven, Jin lost interest in watching it, and it's become harder and harder to find, a tiny rectangle of tape from the days before videos were saved to computers. It's dim, and shows us pacing around and joking about how we'd practiced pinning diapers on a teddy bear. Our faces reflect our joy when Jin finally appears and we hold him, but the film strikes me as conveying so much less than what actually happened. I wore patched pants and walked in circles. We sat with friends who brought us coffee and made anxious chitchat. When the plane pulled up we ran to the window, and later we held Jin, turning and turning, but what actually took place is impossible to describe: it was like someone opened us up at the chest and sewed him in.

We still celebrate that anniversary. Bruce and I give a toast in honor of Jin's birth parents. I used to say simply, "Thank you, you have done a beautiful thing," but as Jin has grown older I see the shadow that crosses his face when he hears this, and I understand that it sounds like I'm thanking them for relinquishing him. I talk to Jin about what his birth parents granted him in this decision, like the ability to go to college and grow up outside of the Korean clan registry system, which would note his illegitimacy, but the privilege of college and the freedom to marry whom he wants and lead a white-collar life as opposed to doing manual labor—the future he faced in Korea unless a family there adopted him—are too abstract for him now.

Now I say, "We remember you," to his birth parents, and leave it at that, thanking them in my mind.

I still page through the photos in the arrival scrapbook with Jin, but he's restless now and doesn't pay attention. For him it's hard to understand being flown somewhere to be given to two strangers, however good everyone's intentions. For a while, when he was little, Jin fantasized that he used to live with his uncle David—whom he scarcely knew at the time—and sent away for Bruce and me, and we came in a package in the mail. He reshaped the tale of being brought to us so that the story launched us, rather than him, into the air, with Jin waiting for us and in control.

Over the course of time I worried about Jin's failure to accept the narrative we spun out for him. By five he'd become a popular kid, busy with neighborhood friends, not thinking about his adoption too much. Or perhaps he struggled with something I could not put my hands on to fix.

～

Always talk about adoption, we were told. Tell him as much as he's able to understand. My son, at ages two and three, heard from us the general story of coming out of a woman's tummy to be born. Like other adopted kids, he heard the story with the coda of the tummy belonging to another woman. At that age, Jin was young enough to lie on my stomach when we took baths together.

"No!" he would holler at me in his formidable small voice. "I came from here!" And he aimed his shoot of a finger at my stomach.

Until a fairly old age, maybe six, Jin loved to pretend to be born. He rolled up under the covers of the bed and called in a squeaky voice, "I hatch out of my egg!" He would ask me to lean on top of him and hatch him. After he rose into a chick, I mimed putting chewed food into his mouth.

For the next few years, Jin remained something—oblivious? resistant?—to the fact of his adoption. He knew many other adopted children. His friend Heidi's young birth mother attended her birthday parties. We celebrated Jin's adoption day. It seemed as if we were putting all the elements in place for him to calmly and naturally see himself as the product of the union of other people's sperm and egg. When he argued with me about his birth, we would show him the video of his arrival at the airport, and whenever we leave from the south satellite of the airport—often, as we travel a lot—we go through the story again.

"There's where we first saw you."

"There's where Daddy thought you were that girl."

"That's where I couldn't move."

Around the age of eight, Jin began asking about his birth parents. Bruce and I shared the little information we had, went over the documents from the adoption agency with their odd little details, like tattoos and the birth order of each of his biological parents. I asked Jin how much he thought about his birth mother.

Some, he said, not all the time.

"How do you feel about it when you do?"

"Sad."

"Sad why?"

"I don't even know what she looks like! It's unfair."

We have a photograph of his foster mother, Mrs. Choi, with Jin in her lap when he was just a few weeks old. I could see him struggling to imagine himself even smaller than that, caught inside the body of someone else. He once told me he remembered his birth mother and her name was Kimchi, actually the name of a dish of pickled vegetables served at every Korean meal, which at that age might have been his clearest symbol of Korea. I hadn't expected it all to be so hopelessly confusing.

"You're sad about this, fragile, right now." I rubbed his back. To me that is saying, Let's erase the separateness, the bodiness between us. He hunched over, still.

Jin was about six when other children first teased him for being different—at least, that was the first time I was around to witness the teasing. I think it must have been spring break; the weather had turned fine and he had the day off from school. We drove to one of our favorite parks, on the edge of an astonishingly beautiful lake carved out of a few of Washington State's smaller mountains. The park had an unused tennis court filled with sand, so we would get in the water, wade around, and head over to the tennis court to build sand castles and get nice and damply sandy. I went a few yards away to retrieve something from the tote bag I always carried, and on my way back saw some boys surrounding Jin as he crouched in the sand.

"Why are you with *her?*" one said.

"You're an orphan," said another one.

"Why are you an orphan? Orphan!" they kept saying; the tone lay between taunt and curiosity.

I ran up, told them I was his mother, period, and they scattered. Then I found the woman supervising them (they were with a group camp) and, characteristically, blew my top. The boys were plenty old enough to know that this was bad behavior, I told her, and demanded an apology. The boys did apologize, then skulked away. I had always imagined a moment like this and understood it would be painful, but I pictured us talking about it, Jin accepting my comfort, as he could at that age, perhaps even appreciating my care for him. I turned to find him huddled over, sobbing.

"Get away from me!" he screamed. His face scrunched, lower lip folded in half. "Get away! If they didn't see you they wouldn't have said anything."

He was in a rage at me. He couldn't forgive me for having been with him, for being who I was. He cried and repeated that I should have just stayed away from him, all the way home. I hurt for him. I hurt, in a way that ripped me apart.

My son would name and rename himself. At five, for a few weeks, he was Harry Potter. Every morning I drew a lightning bolt on his forehead, and he wore a cape we found for him somewhere. Later he became Djinn, pronounced Jin, but spelled to reflect his interest in Arabic stories. Now he has added his original Korean surname, Kim, as a middle name, giving him quite a handle. Whatever name he has, he insists everyone use it—teachers, friends, neighbors—except for us, his parents.

At age eight and a half, Jin changed his name to Penguin S' Ice, and he kept that name for a year and a half, unbratty in his corrections, but adamant. I still don't know what the "S" stood for. The apostrophe was equally vague but definite. When asked what his name was—as kids are half a dozen times a day—he said, "Penguin," or "Penguin S' Ice," with a trace of discomfort but no explanation.

Sometimes people assumed the name was Asian.

"Oh, so that's your original name?" they asked. "What does it mean?"

He responded with an incredulous look. "It means Penguin."

Jin surrounded himself with emblems of his new being—stuffed penguins, plastic penguins, emperor and rockhopper penguins. He had an enormous stuffed penguin named Adulty and a tiny one named Chickie and played penguin parent and child.

At one of those build-a-stuffed-animal workshops, we bought him yet another penguin, designed with a glowing heart and a chip that makes it talk. When we went to pay, the kindly middle-aged saleswoman asked my son his name.

"Penguin," he said.

"Not your doll, honey," she said with a smile, leaning over with her spectacles dangling. "You."

"Penguin," he repeated, knowing this answer would not make sense to her. I could see him choose not to explain himself; she and her spectacles lived in another world. His world was his, giant stuffed emperor penguins lined up against little plastic Adélie penguins in the fort that had overtaken his room that summer, constructed over the months and based around an old TV packing box.

"You know what I hate about grown-ups?" he asked me once. "Grown-ups always want to know what you want to do when you grow up."

My son couldn't, or wouldn't, explain why this disgusted him so much. Perhaps he realized that the kinds of responses he would give—say, designing video games—would meet with condescending smirks. Perhaps he doubts he'll ever be a grown-up, in the sense the speaker uses the term. Or maybe it's just the way adults constantly feel the need to ask children their ages, where they go to school, and what their goals are, as if our young live in a perpetual state of inspection or border crossing.

At the time Jin changed his name, many kids at Jin's school were experimenting with calling themselves other things: Viper, Spring. Jin went to a small and progressive elementary school; kids would wear Santa hats every day for a year, or try eating on all fours. The teachers took whatever didn't disrupt the class in stride.

The kids, without much sense of behavior being off-limits, seemed to keep practicing how to be human again, making a little society from the ground up. I envied them that.

At home, we lived in a boy-blur, five boys his age on our block, all friends off and on, and several more on the next block and around the corner. The neighborhood kids used to hang out in our kind-of-finished basement, which has a Wii and a crooked pool table and a load of old rockers and beanbag chairs. We called it the Crypt or the Underworld.

Jin in late elementary school became aware of himself as different, Asian, in his school environment. The neighborhood friends seemed to be on a different wavelength. When the kids were about ten, I read as they played in my living room, and Jin's friend Jonny mentioned a friend of his who's adopted.

"I'm adopted," said Jin, rather obviously.

"*Really?*" said Jonny. "You're *adopted?*"

I knew that in some sense Jonny must have registered Jin's adoptedness—his features and hair and body type, all so different from mine and his father's—but I also grasped that none of these differences had seemed important enough to him to register consciously, unlike the things that did matter: what snacks we kept in our fridge and cupboards, the fireworks we would buy, the sleepovers out on the trampoline or the games in the Crypt. We simply *were*, in his world, part of the unquestioned nature of things, and this is part of why we have never moved from here.

∽

I remember my son's infancy well, first the days of napping together and baby slings, the smell that's somehow both individual and baby—milk, mild soap. Many things seemed possible: that we would never sleep again, that I would never again have clothing without Mercator maps of pea or tomato stains. But I suppose the arrival of children should clue us in that we must abandon any sense of certainty about how things will unfold. I have been through it with pregnant friends, due dates passing as they rub their stomachs with absent but intimate exhaustion.

Eventually we figured some things out: if you rocked Jin, he went to sleep. If you lay on the floor with him and played Leaning Tower of Baby, he belly laughed. If you gave him a blueberry, he put it between his teeth like a jeweler testing a pearl, then spat it out. After the first year it seemed impossible that I would ever find this beautiful child mysterious.

When he got hungry, we knew what he wanted and could fetch it for him. When he got a little older and cried for my hand or my hair, there wasn't a whole lot of doubt about what to do. I can find those parts of my body, and once he had them, he was happy.

When nothing else worked, we could always let him play with the vacuum cleaner, which he adored. Once, Bruce scheduled salespeople from an upscale vacuum company to visit our house when only Jin and I were home. Jin, eighteen months, climbed onto my lap, jammed his thumb into his mouth, and stared at the two-hour demo of the vacuum and its many parts—along with the accompanying "Dust Mite Video"—with the intensity of someone viewing his own version of porn.

Whatever Jin needed, we had. The whole situation, I think, led to a certain overconfidence on our part.

I suppose I've come around to the beginning of my parenting, to the anxious and delicious waiting and who-is-this-going-to-be? We know these children in the way we know the heavens, basing our knowledge on the lights that arrive in our orbit possibly already extinguished at the source.

I cannot know if he's happy any more than I know why he turned into Penguin. Because he doesn't know. He has nothing to compare his life to, and by the time he can look back with candor and compassion—grown from a baby on a pillow on the seat of an airline—it will be perhaps some time beyond me. Like a star's light, the flickerings of a child's mind may well be gone by the time they reach our understanding. We fumble with our faulty equipment to find that they love dragons as they discover Bionicles and robots. We remember their care for animals as they suddenly become, like a niece of ours, a poet. We besiege their fort with our questions, little harmless arrows breaking against the portcullis. I find myself doing it.

"What did you do in school today?" I slip a few times a week, with a question that, most kids will tell you, can only validly be answered with "Nothing."

$\sim$

At seven, Jin ran a daycare center. He headed a small staff, all of them moss- and muck-bottomed as him, nails brackish-green. They squatted and hovered, prodding their small charges—a nest of roly-polies—into place. The teachers they supervised were a couple of earthworms, who somehow managed to take on the wise, objective, yet approving look of guardians of the young.

Most properly called pillbugs, though sometimes known as potato bugs or potato beetles or even woodlice, roly-polies look like mini-armadillos. Touched, they curl up into an armored ball, a round bullet. They're not beetles, nor are they insects or even arachnids; they're crustaceans, sharing an ancestor with lobsters, crayfish, and shrimp.

Of course, none of these children, in their T-shirts and shorts, thought of their game in terms of twigging little land-lobsters back into their moss enclosure. Bugs, to a kid, are bugs. The daycare lay at the base of an oak tree in Jin's schoolyard, in the damp organic matter pillbugs love. Like earthworms, pillbugs are natural composters, eating what falls to the ground. Mulchers by trade, the earthworms showed no talent for caretaking, letting their charges crawl off on their seven pairs of legs. The children scooped them back and tucked them under leaves. The pillbugs disappeared between school recesses anyway, and had to be replenished.

Jin went to a small Montessori school called Cedar Tree. The school had acquired an old church, with 1960s Pop Art stained glass and a kitchen where the children often cooked, learning to count as they measured, and it had a large yard full of firs and cedars. In this hippie town Montessori schools draw the hippiest of the lot: Jin's schoolmates had names like Bliss and Sequoia and Butterfly. Jin loved the school; he loved his teacher, Kim, and the freewheelingness of it, kids inventing elaborate games and new names, over and above the hopeful and nature-y handles they were given.

Jin and his friend David were masterminds of the daycare. I arrived at school one day to pick up Jin and found them hunched together at the tree, Jin's straight black hair next to David's blond ruckus of curl.

"Not yet," Jin murmured at me, "not yet," speaking I suppose to my shadow, as I hadn't said anything; I just stood behind him, my form intuitable, symptom of a life in which he's constantly moved around. I was in no hurry, and I loved watching the kids: the fingers of a seven-year-old aren't much longer than a pencil stub, and they still have a just-learning fumble. The boys' faces tightened with concentration as they grasped a roly-poly, piled up useless barriers of leaves. Jin continued to murmur to me, seeming to barely hear himself: "I don't want to go yet," and then, "You, go back, you're not supposed to go that far," to a wayward bit of leggy crustacean.

Jin had made friends with David, who remained one of his best friends for many years, after David unaccountably walked up to him at school and punched him hard in the nose. This quality was emerging as a part of Jin's nature; if someone treats him badly, even now, he has a knack for turning the situation around and gaining that person's trust, making him or her a friend. He disarms people with his ability to slow down and understand them.

Girls also huddled around the daycare, though it was the boys I watched, wondering what Shakespeare's Gloucester would think. "As flies to wanton boys are we to the gods," Gloucester says in *King Lear*, "they kill us for their sport." I remember my coiffed aunts, the Greek choruses of my life on all matters of gender, mouthing "boys will be boys," mildly approvingly, at whatever frog-poking or fish-throwing boy-mayhem we girls reported down at the shore, when we went there in the summer.

These boys even remembered the roly-polies' need for amusement; these small, horned BBs were children, in the tiny world of the buggy daycare, children in need of play. They made the Dunk-O-Twig, a tilted twig that could drop a small object to the ground if hit correctly with a pebble; they built little ponds into the daycare grounds. They scraped up oak leaves into beds for napping.

In addition to the cat we have, a gray striped tomcat named Meow-Meow which Jin particularly loves, he has taken on hamsters, rats, even a huge and hairy black spider he named Jaws, who lived in an orb web outside our front door one fall. Jin fed Jaws fruit flies and mosquitoes, critters he was not inclined to mother. He taught Meeko the dog to dance by twirling treats around and around over his head. At the time of his pillbug daycare he wheedled us into getting him a hamster, named Hamtaro, the first in a well-loved but short-lived dynasty. Hamtaro died within a few months for reasons we never figured out, a loss that led to three straight days of crying by my son.

We are born adopting. Nobody demonstrates this better than a child.

~

I met a woman at a writer's conference named Patricia Jabbeh Wesley, who is from Liberia. We talked about our children. She told me that where she comes from, people believe you can be born to more than your biological mother—born to others also, in the spirit world.

"You gave birth to him spiritually," she told me. I told my son this story.

"Meh."

He says that now to everything. I told him once about the Chinese belief that some people come into the world connected to you by an invisible red thread, and they must become part of your life. I pointed out where I thought the thread lay, impossibly thin but unbreakable, between us. I believe he left the room then, not unkindly.

My friend Dawn tells me that maybe we can be born of many people, not just one. Another mother, Karen, told me a story about her adoptive child's birth, which she attended with her husband, Marcus:

"So she's pushing and Marcus and I are holding both of her hands. I see the head, then the baby's born. And the baby's just this little Smurf-blue doll. Alex's mother says, 'Why isn't she crying?' The doctor says, 'The cord is wrapped around her neck, give me a minute.' He has the baby's butt in his hand with the rest of her inverted. Just when I think I should be worried the doc says, 'She's going to breathe now' and Alex just gasped in air and everything turned pink. All of a sudden this doll moved and started whimpering. And I thought, I just witnessed her soul enter her body. I felt that if Marcus and I weren't there, a different soul would have entered her body. I tell people to watch for that moment. That soul is my kid. Nothing could convince me otherwise."

It sounded comforting but not as convincing as I'd like. I forgot these comments about the many people in our lives who make us until I was reading out loud to Jin from a book of Greek myths. I read stories of Zeus's great fight with his father Chronos—why it thunders, to let Zeus's world know he's angry. Why we have to endure winter, our freezing winds traveling down from the Arctic. My son and I both loved these clear, if brutal, explanations of things.

In myth, birth can happen in hundreds of ways: Athena springs from the head of Zeus, Dionysius is born from Zeus's thigh and raised by nymphs, the twins Castor and Pollux, sons of two fathers, hatch from a single egg. Others come from the void and the seafoam.

9.

Age Ten: Mothers and Real Mothers

A T THE AGE of ten, my son kept asking to meet his birth mother. She lives somewhere in the suburbs of Seoul, to the best of our knowledge, and we live an ocean away. Until he turns eighteen, per agency rules, Jin cannot request a meeting with his birth mother or father. We've told him this fact, gently. Still, as we talked about visiting Korea, Jin grew imaginative about how his birth mother might swoop in on us, mother ex machina. We thought about taking a Korea tour with his tae kwon do dojang.

"What if I take a class and she turns out to be the teacher?" he asked me.

"And?" I said. "What do you think would happen?"

We talked about this at night, cuddling on the mattress he has always insisted on keeping on the floor. Jin slept that way by some instinct long before knowing it was a Korean practice to sleep on the floor, which in Korea is gently heated, just as he has always eaten what we'd consider dinner food for breakfast, as Koreans do.

"She would recognize me."

"Then what?"

"She'd be," he groped, "... overjoyed."

She. My husband Bruce and I have always stuck to the term *birth mother.* The phrase feels clunky and impossibly limited, as if you could take all the complexities of a relationship between a man and a woman, nine months of growth, and reduce it to the moment of delivery.

My son followed our practice of saying "birth mother" until around his tenth year, when he occasionally began saying "my mom" to mean his birth mother. It stung me to hear "mom" used to refer to someone else, but I reconciled myself to it more easily than I could have guessed. I imagined what must be happening in his mind—how real this unknown woman, who shared his genes, must be—and accepted it. But if I'm honest with myself, when he asked about his birth mother, I felt uncertain, faced with a relationship of such importance to us both, full of so many questions, and language that felt inadequate to the task of talking it through.

Around this time, Jin developed a deep racial awareness. His self-image became not just of being himself but of being Korean. He began to wish for more kids of color around him and to seek out Asian friends, such as a Vietnamese friend, Gary, and a half-Japanese friend, Angel. Jin took plain white T-shirts and scrawled on them the symbol from the Korean flag—the yin-yang symbol—along with slogans like "Eat My Bibimbap!" and "Seoul Boy." He would not be willing to mark himself as so overtly different a few years later.

～

International Korean adoption began with the Korean War, which killed fathers and impoverished birth mothers. The biracial children fathered by GIs were unwelcome in Korea, with its emphasis on bloodlines and stigmatization of sex outside marriage. But after the 1988 Olympics, held in Seoul, the government of Korea slowed visas for what the law calls "relinquished orphans." Ironically, the reason for this had to do with American news coverage of adoption, which became a constant theme in Olympics coverage: a *New York Times* headline blared "Number One Export: Babies." Korea lost face, so the international adoption policy was changed. By 2011, the number of visas issued by Seoul for overseas adoption amounted to 736, less than half of what it had been just a few years prior, in 2004.[13]

While officially the government of Korea balanced the restriction on overseas adoption by promoting adoption at home, in reality that effort has largely failed. The country's major newspaper, the *Korea Times*, has called for an end to the quota system on visas for international adoptions, citing the fact that currently only about a quarter of children in Korean orphanages will find homes each year. Declaring that it's "time to scrap the overseas quota system" and referencing domestic "prejudice and discrimination against adoption," the editorial also called for greater social support for unwed mothers.

In the 1990s, China and Russia overtook Korea as the countries of origin of most internationally adopted American children. Now, some African countries are showing the greatest growth in international adoption—Ethiopia, Sierra Leone, Malawi, and others. Sub-Saharan Africa is home to an astonishing thirty-four million orphaned children, eleven million of them due to AIDS alone.

◦—

After calling his birth mother "mom" in some casual contexts, Jin began to refer to her as "my real mom." I swallowed my heart back down for a long second, though he tossed the phrase off easily.

A friend of mine, with an adopted daughter a little younger than Jin, mentioned that her Marie had just used the phrase "my real mom" as well.

"I was going to correct her," my friend said. "Then I thought, who am I to tell her who her real mother is?"

I considered my friend's question. I asked Jin to tell me what made a mother "real." He mumbled something about genes and giving birth. I remembered the thousands of changed diapers, the tantrums, earaches, late-night visits to the ER (one screamy three-hour wait was so awful that Bruce and I turned cheerleader: "Scream, honey! Come on, scream! Get them in here!").

And the greater fact of learning how little all that matters, how easy it is after all to go without sleep, and a love that feels as if it might liquefy you at any minute.

I decided that in my presence Jin could designate us Real Mom One and Real Mom Two, in whatever order he chose.

Which likely comes close to how he thinks.

Another night, snuggling up to his pillows with his coterie of stuffed animals around us, Jin asked about finding "his mom" again.

"But we don't have her address. We don't know where she lives," I reminded him.

"How could you not know more about my mom? You're the mom," he whined.

⟿

I think of Jin's birth parents all the time, as he grows into his adult face, cheeks slimming and features moving farther apart, stretched and grown up. He is a palimpsest for them, a beautiful canvas that shows traces of the artists and artwork that preceded it. I live with them as I live with him and I know them as a vital part of my life, people I love through what they made together, though I may never meet them. I've always suspected that when Jin makes contact with his birth parents, he'll want to do that on his own, without adoptive parents around to complicate matters. Of course, he may not search or succeed in finding them at all.

Many adopted children want to find their birth parents, though when I researched this question, wondering how Jin might feel one day, kids who search turned out to be fewer than I had imagined; in one large study of adult Korean adoptees, about 37 percent wanted to search, while 29 percent did not want to. Among those with a desire to search, curiosity and medical information led the list of reasons.[14] It is not, in other words, always a question of searching for birth parents as a way of resolving questions about identity. I've encouraged Jin to think of searching for his birth parents as a positive thing, even as I understand that his desires, and the outcome of a search, live outside my control.

Jin asked again and again what his birth mother's circumstances were, what might have been going on with her besides being young, unmarried, and underpaid as a waitress in an expensive city and a Confucian culture that did not allow illegitimate children access to college and white-collar employment. I stressed her youth, the loving gift of bearing a child when there are options, and at some point said something like, "We all have points in our life when we're just not ready to be parents." Jin's face fell in on itself.

"You mean she didn't *want* me?"

"No, no, I'm sure she did, but she couldn't make it work," I said, and fumbled trying to answer questions about unanswerable things.

I see glimpses of a feeling that's somewhere between sadness and worry on Jin's face when we talk about his birth mother. At other times he hunches over, sad and silent in a way he never is otherwise, as if some part of his history lies clenched in his throat. It will form a struggle for him, one he already faces with a degree of casual heroism I admire terribly. At times it can bring me to tears.

⁓

A month or two after we began our talks about the term "real mom," Jin had a tantrum. He stomped up the stairs.

"You're unfair!"

I went up to calm him and put him to bed. As I slipped in beside him he said, "You're unfair! You've always been unfair! I'm going to get a lawyer. I'm going to sue you and go back to my real parents in Korea."

"We are real," I said. "We love you and give you food and clothes and a place to live and make your lunches. Your birth parents are very important but we're real parents." It all sounded so far from the point. Then I said something like: I'm upset and I need to go now and I love you.

As I headed to the door, Jin sprang up and grabbed me around the waist.

"I'm so sorry," he said. "You can't go. I love you." He had never apologized like this, ever. He had frightened himself and I guess I frightened him too. His fear bothered me more than his threat. I went back to his bed with him.

After our usual—books and songs—we talked about his words again.

"Real parents love you unconditionally," I told him. "That means no matter what you do, we love you."

"Really?" He'd heard this before but had never connected with the idea. "You mean if I robbed a bank?"

"Yeah. I would wish you hadn't done it, but I would love you."

Jin's hypothetical questions grew more and more baroque, spiraling from larceny all the way to becoming Adolf Hitler.

"Yes," I told him, "if you did what Adolf Hitler did, I would still love you. I would hate what you did but I would love you."

"You'd love me if I were Adolf Hitler?" He paused to think. "That's scary."

I suppose it is scary, though we don't think of that, with our faith in unconditional love. Love can scare you, when you realize it can take you to places you never thought you could go: knowing you have it in you to love even what you cannot pardon, and to love what can leave you.

My own fear came less from hearing Jin say those words I had thought would come as unimaginably painful—"I'm going back to my real mom"—than it did from my reaction. I had imagined this as the moment that would test my parenting more than any ear infection or endless night-night car or hair pulled out to wrap around a thumb: the moment that would cause the mothering tears to flow like nothing else, the moment that motherhood itself, with all its passions and its pains, got ripped away. After an hour or two, though, it didn't hurt really, as I felt my perspective shift again, Jin's vision overriding mine. If Jin grows up and needs to be somewhere else, have someone else answer, singly, to the title of mother, I can accept even that.

This is scary love, that allows this possible ending to the story.

10.

Age Eleven:
All of the Above

W HEN WE BOUGHT this house of ours, this tiny Victorian in Bellingham on the Washington coast, I thought of it as somewhere to be until we got a little older and bought a place out in the country with more land, with fruit trees for me, maybe even chickens. But our street has evolved into a community; we've come to share each other's kids and lives, and we have parties, including a huge block party complete with fireworks on the Fourth of July. As much as the kids squabble, Jin has sworn he will never leave here. Bruce and I were asked to apply for a pair of better jobs in Virginia a few years ago, with more pay in a cheaper place to live, and when we tried to talk to Jin about moving he became hysterical and sobbed for an hour straight.

"But I thought you were mad at everybody!" I made the mistake of saying. Jin had had one of those weeks when all of the boys in the neighborhood had been bickering and bickering, banging on each other's doors in between swearing they'd never speak to one another again.

"I didn't mean it! I didn't mean it!"

As Bruce and I thought about those better jobs, with their higher pay and lower mortgages, Jin made the move completely out of the question by sobbing about the garden.

"What about Mama's garden? What about the Magic Garden? What about that?" His breath heaved. "We can't take that with us."

This particular plea struck us dumb. Jin sat at our dining room table, wracked and doubled over. I could see his face, scrunched and wet as an infant's.

"Okay," Bruce and I said, no doubt at almost the same time. "We won't go."

All three of us love our garden, though I never would have guessed Jin cared that much about it, that it would rank even above leaving his friends in his list of reasons to stay in Bellingham. It's an English cottage garden that breeds weeds in the wash of blues, pinks, and purples from tulips, irises, lupines, delphinium. Some plants I put in only because they appear in Shakespeare and I love saying their names aloud: rue, columbine, fennel. Some I just love the names of, like feverfew, and their histories: this plant with daisy-like flowers has an almost medicinal odor, citrus crossed with bleach, and used to be strewn across the floors of sickrooms to counter the smell of illness.

Jin and I started our habit of calling our garden the Magic Garden. Jin named it this during the summer the snapdragon appeared, when he was ten or so, but we should have known the garden for what it was during the summer of the foxgloves. A nephew of ours had been diagnosed with leukemia several years before that summer, and through the pummeling of his body with chemo and radiation, he'd been left with a weakened heart. He had been put on digitalis, a drug derived from foxgloves. We heard the news from my brother-in-law and the next day I walked out to the side of my house and found it drooping with foxgloves. I somehow hadn't noticed the plants as they shot up, and they opened their flowers all at once: the speckled tubular blooms just the size and color to grace a fox's paws.

"I want snapdragons," Jin said on a walk the following summer. I understood: I remember some overwhelming comfort as a child in putting my finger into a snapdragon's jaw.

"Okay, sometime," I told him, making a mental note to buy some snapdragons. Next day I found a yellow one tangled in a hanging branch of rose in my front yard. I ran and got Jin.

"Wow, cool!" We opened the little yellow mouths and praised the garden's gift of anticipating us.

"It's a magic garden, Mom," Jin explained, and we've called it that ever since. It has produced, on a wish, campanula, an orgy of Day-Glo poppies at the side of the back yard, and white lilac.

A skeptical view of our Magic Garden would be that Jin and I saw those wished-for plants all along—the foxglove, the snapdragon—but registered them only when they became meaningful. I'm no skeptic, though, nor is Jin, and we find the wisdom of magic no less true than easy pragmatics. There is a magic inherent in community, in love, in being where we're meant to be and not in Virginia or anywhere else, as there is in realizing you already have what you want.

Many of the flowers in my garden started life as the flowers of my neighbors, and vice versa; we share everything, and Rob or Gene appearing at my door with a shovel and a request to dig some perennials happens all summer. The kids know they can pop in at any house. They know the rhythms of adults intimately, even if they are indifferent to our secrets—our little fights within the family, the private cultures of our households: who eats dinner together, which kids do homework first. Jin has a Japanese American friend a few blocks away, and an adopted biracial girl around the corner. The families have many shades of difference: divorce, swing shifts, many patterns of arrival and departure.

Yet even so, Jin would say occasionally, "I don't want to be Asian and adopted. I want to be like everybody else. I hate being different."

Once, when we ate in one of British Columbia's Koreatowns, Jin said he wanted our neighborhood to stay exactly as it is but be in Korea, with everyone in it Korean. "Like, Tom would be Korean," he said of a friend his age, and, "Can you imagine a Korean *Gene?*"

Gene is the reckless, feckless guy across the street, a bearded mile-a-minute talker who loves to blow things up. Gene started the tradition of detonating his old Christmas trees on the Fourth of July, and now has a yard full of Christmas trees drying out— most from neighbors, but also one that he and Jonny filched from a Boy Scout truck—waiting to be wired up in the summer with fireworks synchronized by cannon fuses.

"I come from the best town there is," Jin said to me recently.

"Bellingham?"

"No, Seoul."

Jin's small school has a large number of adoptees and diversity, with kids whose parents came from China, India, Russia, Togo, Nepal. Racism has come up—more as he's gotten to middle school age—but not to the extent it would elsewhere.

Jin is aware, with a casual clarity, of his own color, in a way that's surprised me at times, and that's evolved. He rooted desperately for Barack Obama to become president.

"I want someone with brown skin in the White House," he told me matter-of-factly. It's clear to him that some people don't like those with brown skin. And that for many, he fits into that category.

Bruce and I both believed, for the longest time and with the optimistic naivety of parents, that Jin's popularity would somehow glide over issues of race. The many kids in our neighborhood attached themselves to Jin, taking an old playhouse in our yard and making it into a clubhouse. They sold lemonade for supply money, choosing their street corner with great care and earning $25 in the first half hour. I poked my head into the clubhouse one day and found a crimson snapdragon in the window box, a tiny but lovely wicker credenza, and a perfectly hammered-in brass doorknocker.

Then, when he was eleven, Jin was mocked by a boy his age, a friend of Jin's friend Mario. This boy, Robert, called Jin

"Chopsticks" and "China Boy" and other names, and he called Mario "Fat Mexican." Though, according to Jin, this name-calling is normal for Robert and Mario, a chronic bullying that occurs somehow within the zone of a friendship, Jin felt angry and upset. He came home from Mario's house and sat down, not crying or ranting, just mad at Robert. He told us the story easily, between bites of fusilli, which would not have been the case if he'd been hurt or shamed badly—then, he would have come home very emotional and only slowly told us the reason.

Bruce nonetheless said of Robert, "I'd like to wring his little neck."

A few days later Jin told me, "When Robert started calling us names, we called him names. We said, 'Oh, White American Boy, hamburger, hamburger.'" Jin re-created the moment with a funny eye roll and shimmy.

I couldn't decide how I felt about that. Making up your own racial slurs isn't exactly constructive. On the other hand, sensing that Robert's race too posed vulnerabilities—wasn't that progress? Even reporting it, Jin laughed at his own wit.

"Isn't talking about things better?" I said finally, whereon Jin said, "We didn't call names till he did. And it's better than having Daddy wring his little neck."

I couldn't argue with that.

⌒

When Jin was six, we took a trip to Macon, Georgia, where Bruce grew up. Bruce wanted his son to see the places that had been important to him as a boy, and to learn the lessons of the Old South. We took Jin to see the "Whites" and "Coloreds" drinking fountains preserved at the old Macon train station, and to Baconsfield Park, which had been willed to the city by a senator "for," as he stated it, "the benefit of white women and children." Bruce, as a child, had played at Baconsfield Park when it was legally segregated—swinging on swings and building forts with his twin brother.

Jin knew—we had always told him—that he is not white. He knew that many groups of people exist—ethnicities, races, religions—and by birth he is Korean. We had told him that we were all now Italian and Southern and West Indian and Korean and other things together, because we were a family. That was our truth, inside our world: our walls, our family society, our neighborhood. But here we faced the image of Senator Bacon, whose plantation-style home still stood across the street. And here lay a harder truth.

"Would I have been allowed to play at Baconsfield Park?" Jin asked us. We found ourselves strangely surprised and stymied by the question. It's hard to imagine Tom and Steven and Kyler and Nick and Jonny and Luke racing through Baconsfield Park, with Jin on the other side of the street, heartsick.

"No, probably not," we told Jin, along with what we could think of to make sense of this odd fact: that Senator Bacon would not even have been thinking of Asians (did that make it any better?), that he had forgotten to stipulate white men as well as women and children so Daddy too would be out on a technicality, that as someone whose grandfather was born in the West Indies I might not have been allowed into Senator Bacon's park either.

⌒

When Jin was ten, one of his teachers praised his "one-half Korean, one-quarter New Yorkan, and one-quarter Southern" way of summing up his identity. When Janine, the teacher, told me that formula, it was news to me: I had never heard Jin put his heritage that way before, and when I asked Jin how he calculated it, he shrugged.

Janine said, "It seemed so healthy, to integrate everything that way." It was healthy. Jin used that all-of-the-above formula— sometimes substituting "Italian" for "New Yorkan"—until he hit his teens.

I look at my boy sometimes and think that being a dual minority—in race and in family formation—is a lot for him to carry on his slim shoulders. Once I described my grandfather, his great-grandfather, coming here from Barbados and he wailed, "I am too many things!" If only all that mattered was the matching of a parentless child with a child-wanting parent. But these complications—of birth and parentage and ethnic identity and skin color, which in many cultures have simply not mattered— do matter in our world, and are our dilemmas to wrestle with.

The complexities of race are real, but the simplicity of parenting is real too: the joy of loving children. One day, as Jin's friends streaked through our yard, Bruce and I talked about how there was not a child there we could not easily take in and love, if it came down to it. I have cared for every child on my street, wiped their butts and noses, met many of them the day they came home from the hospital or birthing center. I have fed them and their parents have fed me. We are Italian, New Yorkan, Korean, Washingtonian, Bellinghaman, part of one another.

11.

Age Twelve: Hosts

F OR SEVERAL YEARS, when Jin was a preteen, we attended
a Korean Baptist church. Jin had started taking tae kwon do
lessons at the age of six, and the dojang and some friends here
and there served as our main link to the local Korean community. One day at the dojang, Jung, the mother of a Korean
American girl named Katie, approached me and wrote out the
address of the church. Jung pressed the paper into my hand and
said something about how they would like us to come, would like
to have Jin see how Koreans meet together and worship and eat,
all elements of the Korean Sunday service. Bruce and I had been
looking for ways to help Jin feel more integrated with Koreans in
Bellingham, so, though Bruce and I remained Catholic, we went
one Sunday, and kept going, in love with the group.

My son at twelve was resolutely not Catholic. He believed
in the Greek and the Roman gods: Jupiter, Athena. He favored
Poseidon and Ares, but liked them all. He could tell intricate
stories, like the one about Baucis and Philemon, an old couple

who took in Mercury and Jupiter disguised as travelers. A thousand villagers had turned the gods away, and a thousand were punished. The old couple gave the gods all the hospitality their poverty could offer, even wiping their aged table with mint. Of course, Baucis and Philemon had a great reward: priesthoods in life, preserved together for eternity.

Jin and I decided that he was a classical polytheist. It distinguished him from our coastal Northwest hippie town's many New Age pagans, who believe in a loose polytheism—whales as spirits, firs as spirits, even aliens as spirits—and with whom he did not want to be associated at all. In spite of Jin's Olympian obsessions, we all went to the Korean church. I suppose when we went he sat there and thought his own thoughts.

My family speaks very little Korean, though we've tried many times to learn. The adults at this tiny church spoke little English, while the kids had grown into that language and lost the old one. It was a two-tone Babel. The children had their service in English, led by a man in his twenties with a guitar. Pastor Kim also spoke to the kids briefly, in bits of English mixed with Korean. The first week we went, he told them to insert the Holy Spirit into themselves like a game cartridge, so it would become part of their operating system—*Nintendo-inmida*, "to do Nintendo," we heard him say. The kids would then go into another room where they snuck candy from some occult source and played foosball.

Then the adult service began: women dressed beautifully in suits, with Chanel handbags and hair upswept or held back in jeweled barrettes, and the men all wearing jackets. "*Kituinmida*," intoned Pastor Kim: "Let us pray." We did get that phrase down. Most of what he said settled in our ears as a chant, repetitive at the end of the sentence and rising in pitch, as Koreans place verbs at the last position and these generally end on vowels. Because we knew our Bible well enough, some words emerged— "Absalom," the preacher said one Sunday, and while we were meant to understand we needed to behave like David, not Absalom, Absalom's was the only name I could make out. So for an hour and a half, under the track lighting, sitting on a folding chair, I thought about Absalom the wicked, who tried to take over, even betraying his father.

We heard some things in church because of borrowings from English—*crossinmida*, to do the Cross, to be crucified, as I understood it. *Yes-su Cristo*, Jesus Christ. Mostly we sat, praying and standing and bowing our heads when others did, in the hallucinatory murmur, cadence of end vowel and rising pitch, Lord and Father, Chonim and Abaji.

The Korean church members felt for us. Korean church services run long—an hour and a half at least—and at the end the preacher gamely and haltingly tried to explain in English what he had been preaching about. We were not to be Absaloms, he told us, though I did nothing through that service but try to remember all I could about Absalom or think a dreamy nothing, studying the curves and angles of *hangul*, the Korean alphabet, strung along the wall.

I wanted to tell the pastor there was no need for this explanation: let everyone scoop their children from the foosball. He had succeeded in what he wanted to do. Once, Pastor Kim began gesticulating toward a TV screen set up in the front of the room and I recognized Susan Boyle, breakout star of *Britain's Got Talent*. I knew the drill: get the congregation interested by bringing in topical things, pop culture. I have never liked hearing a priest begin with a story of the latest television, or something funny his little nephew said at Thanksgiving. Those stories are not the ones we're here for.

What did the gods say to Baucis and Philemon? They sat in the couple's cottage for a long time, Jupiter and Mercury, the caduceus disguised as a walking stick, their clothes torn, feet filthy, playing the role of vagrants. The gods seem to have done these things to amuse themselves. They watched as Baucis made a fire from twigs, Philemon cut a piece of fatty pork and simmered it with vegetables and herbs. They ate olives, Ovid says, and dried figs. Did the gods mention how hot the weather had been lately, how Sparta had outrun Athens in an improbable last plunge? Baucis and Philemon, who grew their food and raised a little livestock, probably mentioned how the year had been for their crops. Ovid details the food meticulously but skips over the conversation. It's okay: the gods came for good cheer and small talk. And for the couple's piety—no doubt the two asked the gods to join them in consecrating their simple meal to those whom they were in fact about to feed.

Of course, regardless of our poor Korean, the Bible is the Bible and the stories we heard were stories we knew. So nothing would have completely surprised us. Jesus didn't water-ski in the book of Mark, we knew, and God didn't wear funny hats. The apostles would still sleep in the garden, in Korean.

Members of the congregation—sometimes men, but usually women—stood up from time to time, praying and crying. Some women came in before the service to pray, and they sat in metal chairs, swaying backward and forward, and keened in a deep monotone pulled from someplace below the vocal cords and even the heart. They reminded me of images of Mary, the sway picked up from a motion left in the ether, the keen a broad ontological distress.

"It seems weird at first," Katie, daughter of Jung, confided to Jin about the keening, "but you get used to it."

My husband mentioned to me that people treated him as crazy for going to a church where he didn't know the language. I get that reasoning; I thought it might be crazy too. The first time we went to the Korean church—which I can't even name for you properly, because the name is written on the sign outside and in the bulletins in *hangul*—I expected to listen to ten minutes of language-blur, burning with self-consciousness, and flee. But to be where we were felt more like prayer than prayer, and made language seem like adding on your fingers, something to be used in order to be finally put out of the way. Saint John of the Cross wrote that ultimately "even the act of prayer and communion, which was once carried on by reflections and other methods, is now wholly an act of loving." It's not new to think of mystical knowing and language as separate. It's a strange premise to take to church, with its sermon and print bulletins and writing on the wall.

At the end of our service we turned to one another and said, "I something you, I forgive you, I love you," in Korean.

I've never understood the first part, and I used to hear the formula as ending not with "I love you"—"*saranghayo*"—but with "I am a person, I am only human"—"*saramhayo*." This is pretty garbled Korean, it turns out, as *saramhayo* would mean something like "I person you," though I confidently told my version to my husband.

Then we ate. The women had not only dressed impeccably, they lugged in cookers full of steamed rice, spicy chicken, bulgogi, cold seaweed soup. We filed into a kitchen set up with long, chipped tables, and they would not let Bruce and me fix our own plates, piling everything in bowls for us as if we were infants. They didn't even believe my hot tongue. *Tashee, tashee,* I begged for more *gochu jang,* more pepper paste. You see, like Ovid, I can tell you everything about the food.

Sometimes my son, the happy pagan, seemed to feel the need to hear my name at that age.

"Mom."

"Yes?"

"Mom."

"What?"

"Mom."

"Jin."

"Mom."

"That's my name. Don't wear it out."

If I looked at him, I wouldn't see a desire to tease me or bug me or much more than a half-blank look, a need to throw this verbal ball out and have me catch it. It was vital, I knew, that

I answer. I could say absolutely anything. He was lobbing for a presence caught in that antique and comfortable sound.

Ovid includes a strange touch at the end of the story of Baucis and Philemon. The gods revealed themselves slowly, causing the wine to refill itself in the bowl. When the couple realized whose presence they stood in, they threw themselves to the floor, begging apology. They had one other source of meat: a goose they had raised, improbably, to guard their hovel. They begged permission to kill the watch-goose and provide better, then took off in chase of the bird. But Ovid tells us that "quick-winged, it wore the couple out"—not surprising, since he'd noted that Baucis's old breath was barely able to raise fire from her twigs. What the gods did while the old couple taxed themselves with pursuing a goose he does not say. One hopes they did not find the whole thing too funny. When the goose ran to take shelter with the gods, Jupiter and Mercury called a halt to the madness and gave the couple their reward.

How did the Romans, I wonder, read Ovid's story? Offer the best hospitality to whoever comes along, no matter how impoverished? Chase your geese? They too had a metaphoric understanding. Baucis and Philemon's story tells how to be a guest, taking what is offered kindly, not eyeing the fat fowl. When we mentioned how hard we had been trying to learn Korean, Jung insisted on teaching us, meeting us in the church dining room on Saturdays, using a children's book. "The shoe," we read. "The kitten." Nothing theological. She was patient with us as we did our *hangul* strokes wrong, right to left or down to up rather than the opposite. It was very hard for us to believe that she and the others wanted to do these things for us, as I could see it was hard for them to believe that we wanted to be there, in the shaped silence. We are none of us gods.

Jin used to say the reason he believed in the pantheon is that he didn't believe God could be everywhere. One god is not enough; he dreams of many. I get that, I told him. It's hard to imagine. And if you can't imagine it—I didn't say this—what stories you choose will trouble you anyway. That goose. Either the gods did not have the wherewithal to stop the chase, or it proved the vehicle by which they amused themselves at the expense of old people who'd laid beds for their exhaustion. Perhaps pain baffled the gods. Or joy in their creations' earnest absurdity formed a love of sorts.

I thought of Baucis and Philemon on Sundays, with women handing us plates of rice, spiced celery, bowls of soup with meat. The aroma of the food drifted in all through the service: sweet-soy chili sauces, sesame oil. I can imagine the odor of spearmint rising from the table, pork cooking with rosemary and oregano. Baucis and Philemon even heated water and drew the gods a very human bath for their soiled bodies, water that, as Greeks, they might have scented with bay or juniper. I smell mint all spring and summer, and honeysuckle, roses, lilies, herbs, through the night from my bed. We keep the window open when the garden comes on, sweet pour, a wordless thing, a gift of summer and of life, and of the labor of hands.

We attended the Korean Baptist church until it became riven by conflict. The pastor and the congregation had a falling-out, one which, with our poor Korean, Bruce and I never quite made sense of, except that it seemed to have to do with whether to use the church's money to pay the pastor more or to buy land. We kept in touch with Jung, flew to Korea with our former pastor on the plane, and mourned the loss of the community. I felt as if, to them, my family had been a mission: teaching Jin about Korea and all things Korean, giving us as much of the language as they could. We had never let Jin tell the adults at the church that he believed in the Greek and Roman gods; it would have horrified them. Though the story Jin told me, of the old couple, came close to explaining how they took us in, and why.

12.

Age Twelve: Embarking

TIME BEGAN TO careen, at my son's nearly teen age. I turned the garden back into the earth in October and the next instant found myself picking collard leaves the size of platters and toadflax and daisies and lupines for the dinner table. Mount Baker hid behind the early nighttime and the rain, then reappeared, alive with sun on the snow during the day and alpenglow at sunset. Winter and summer: more and more, morning and afternoon, one moment to another.

Jin, on the verge of the great turn toward adulthood, became fascinated by the concept of growing up. I picked him up at middle school one day. I was heading down one of those streets that are full of lanes kinking off to the side and people cutting in. Jin was full of questions, not noticing my distraction.

"Mom."

"Mmmmmm."

"I wonder how it feels to be an adult."

A woman with a cell phone at her ear swerved at me, and I hesitated.

"Does it feel like, like time goes by in a second?"

I told Jin, being bored still feels like boredom, slow and heavy, but time goes by really fast. Thinking, that's why we waste so much of our time on earth saying, I can't believe I'm a mother. I can't believe I'm a mother of a child who walks. Who speaks. Who goes on his own to a friend's house down the block. Who's in middle school. So much elaborate time expressing how fast time goes.

$\sim$

Jin went on a school trip at twelve, an astonishing five days gone, over to the Columbia River to camp, study Native museums, geology and geography, Lewis and Clark, squeezed with his classmates into a couple of vans.

When it came time for Jin to leave his feelings went back and forth, excited but worried about homesickness, asking me how much I would miss him (to the Big Bang and back I said, needing some drastic measure), offering kisses. Secretly I thought five days to be adults with my husband would be a good thing. When that five days started, though, it turned out to be a miserable thing. The first day of Jin's absence I burst into tears at the weather forecast I heard on the TV at the doctor's office. Rain. My baby sleeping out in the rain.

I did even worse at home, where the walls crowded around

an empty space. It made me wish Bruce and I were at a river. At least the daily rituals—the phone calls and boys pounding on the door that started every day at three, *The Simpsons* at eight—wouldn't feel so gone. Days without Jin bloated, fat with time. Five days in a tent with three boys Jin liked—playing the card game Flux, trading gum—and he was going to see that this won't be so hard, this work of leaving us. While this work of launching him into the world, even in the best ways, will be hard, harder than we thought. The house, the one Jin has told us we're never allowed to sell, will lean into his shape, always.

I sent him an email. He had looked to me to cry when we dropped him off at the school van the morning of the trip.

"Are you going to cry? Are you crying, Mom?"

He knew all my crying stories well: when we first took him to the Little Gym for an hour; his first day at preschool; the day his pediatrician diagnosed pneumonia and asthma. Somehow I didn't cry the morning he left for the river. He didn't have email in his tent on the Columbia, but I thought he might want to get something when he returned.

It's Monday afternoon, the first day of your trip to the Columbia River, & I really miss you. I've been teary all day. I know you won't get this till you get back but I thought I'd send it anyway. I love you. Mom

In seconds an answer came, in Jin's atrocious spelling, and the name he had started to use at times.

Subject: im gone

From: jin woo kim

Sent: Monday, October 19, 2009 10:05 AM

To: Susanne Antonetta

It's an autoreply. Jin's use of "Kim" hurt Bruce's feelings; we gave Jin Bruce's surname. I've heard stories about false information in Korean birth narratives. I warned Jin that "Kim" might be a name somebody picked out of a hat. I don't think he really cared. It's a way to feel attached to the many Korean Kims we know, including Pastor Kim, and in a larger way, to the country where he first drew breath.

The year of the school camping trip we had another El Niño year in the Pacific Northwest, much like the one the infant Jin arrived to. The unruly ocean dawdled at the equator, piling up a bowl of warmth to bring back to us. I picked tomatoes on the 20th of October and sauced them with fresh shallots and marjoram. There were lettuce, fennel. Chrysanthemums just beginning to open. The anniversary of Jin's arrival came in a month, and much like Jin's first year, I'd barely worn a topcoat. It's rare to see the sun here after the start of October, and with the double glow of the sun and its alpine mirror, and twinned blue of sky and sea, the fall colors—gold and red maples and yellow chestnuts—popped against the eye, primary and loud, like crayons or a child's toys.

Someone strange kept writing me emails that fall. She used my name, was me. She begged me for my bank account number, wanting, she said, to send me money. One day this cyber Susanne

Antonetta contacted me with other things on her mind: "We know," her subject line told me, "why you live." Interesting, because we here at S.A. headquarters often felt we don't have a clue why we live. The email's like a dream, Bruce told me. We narrate the dream but have no idea how. The dream knows all about us but we know nothing of the dream.

∽

Adeul. (Son.) *Saranghayo.* (I love you.) Perhaps you were the *we* who knows all about me. First we found each other at an airport. Then you were embarked by me, sent off from me, like the ships I see every day heading off, skating west along the Pacific. Sails like dropped triangles of white paper. Off to explore where Captain George Vancouver did, the man who charted our coastline in the 1700s. Vancouver, like me, was bipolar. As captain, he had the prerogative of naming the to-him new lands, and his mood disorder and captain's privilege flamed out in a rash of names showing how much, to him, everything throbbed with feeling. We live in the flux of him: Restoration Point to Deception Pass and then, Desolation. The Alaskan nostalgia that took his mind back to the places and people of a childhood he must have barely remembered: Lynn Canal, Point Bridget, Point Mary.

Son. Perhaps you thought of me at the river, in a wash of color and light. Perhaps you heard about Lewis and Clark charting the West of America, on foot and in canoes, and it reminded you that many people—not just you—cross strange territories to wind up in the places where they find themselves.

13.

Age Thirteen: Going Back

I N SEPTEMBER OF 2010, we did what we had been promising Jin for years: we flew to Korea to spend two weeks in the country of his birth—the place where he had believed he lived when he shipped himself a parcel of parents.

Jin had turned thirteen in June, a few months before our trip. He was heading into eighth grade, and he'd grown a lot that year. Overnight, it seemed, rather than being the two and a half people we'd been visually for so long, my family stood eye to eye and we couldn't tell our blue jeans and T-shirts apart any longer. All three of us had become the exact same size, five feet six. Jin's face and tummy kept some of the puffiness typical of middle school boys, but the adult he was in the process of turning into had begun making surprise appearances: in a sudden note of baritone where there had been only soprano, in a moment when he went into the kitchen, rummaged through the fridge for tortillas and cheese, and cooked himself a meal rather than asking us to do it. At the same time, Jin in many ways still clung to childhood. He kept the Beatrix Potter bunny wallpaper I kept trying to replace; he still occasionally liked to be told stories or sung to sleep. We lay in our bed, the three of us, to watch TV together, something Jin in a year would find too much closeness.

I remembered the feeling, when Jin was a baby, of seeing the person he was rising at me, closer and closer, as if surfacing in water. I felt this again. A few years before the Korea trip, Jin started making short films when hanging out with friends. He grew more and more serious about making films, and by thirteen he started teaching himself how to film against a green screen and use special effects, do stop-motion animation and Claymation. Jin learned both filmmaking and Web design at this age largely by finding free online tutorials he could focus on, forehead tight with concentration, for hours, though reading a book for school or doing a little bit of homework would bring yowls of misery. We sent him to a few summer day camps doing film, but he already knew most of what they taught.

Jin and Jonny, his favorite friend to film with, created a production company and began posting the movies they made on YouTube: stop-motion films where Jonny appears and disappears and walks through fences, a Claymation movie Jin made by himself, using a halogen lamp he bought himself for the lighting, and an old camping cooler turned on its side as the home of his clay characters. Modeling clay, tripods, and money for better and better cameras became the whole of his lists for Christmases and birthdays.

At thirteen Jin couldn't wait, more than anything, to experience the high-tech side of Korea.

~

We had a social network of families with adopted children from
Korea, and I had always envied those who had flown to Korea
to pick up their children; they talked about the fish markets in
Buson and the street life in Seoul, the babies lying in their identi-
cal cribs at the orphanage, with such an easy intimacy. We had
many Korean friends. But this country, which counted for so
much in my son's biography and in the lives of his very real, yet
unknown other set of parents, I had never seen. I had imagined
visiting Korea throughout Jin's life with us, running through
versions of the story: Jin and I holding each other as we landed,
a vision of arriving in Korea I spun in the optimistic baby days
when you cannot imagine this child ever pulling away from you;
then later, Jin seeing the land of his birth and resenting us for
taking him from it, a thought that gnawed at me as he turned
more teenage and more distant.

Jin grew tense and irritable in the weeks before we left for
Korea, much more so than had been usual for him that summer. If I asked him the simplest thing—to keep his cell phone
on so I could be in touch, to tell us where he was going—he'd
snap at me.

"I don't have to listen to you!" he kept yelling, and glared
meaningfully at me each time he said it, for a second or two.

I could sense his reaching toward "because you're not my real mom." He wore the phrase on his face. He sat at the table a few nights, eating noisily, slamming his plate, but refusing to speak, for no clear reason.

I tried to talk to Jin about how he was feeling, but he shut me out. The prospect of traveling through Korea—with Jin's non-Korean parents and the barrier of the language, which in spite of our church's and another tutor's best efforts still didn't amount, for any of us, to much more than the ability to order in a restaurant—felt overwhelming, full of the possibility of feeling painfully divided from the place where he was born.

"You know," I said, "we have friends like Brian and Andrew and Jung. We have the church. Korea's going to feel like home to you."

Jin spun on his heels out of the room.

⌒

As it happened, our flight to Seoul was delayed by almost a day. The airline announced the delay in one-hour increments for seven hours, warning passengers not to leave the gate area, so we sat on our plastic seats and got hungrier and hungrier. Finally the airline's announcer—who had gone from perky to snappish and monosyllabic during the long wait—came on and told us to line up for hotel vouchers; we weren't going anywhere till tomorrow. The voucher line took another hour and a half of waiting, until we received the scrawled bit of paper and got shunted off to a hotel shuttle. We grabbed some food and a couple hours of sleep in a cheap room we barely noticed, then took a shuttle back at five in the morning to SeaTac Airport, as we'd been instructed to do, a shuttle to the place where our baby had come to us more than a decade before. We waited at the gate for several more hours before our plane finally had a departure time listed, and several more after that before it took off.

The dreamy and emotional flight to Seoul I had always pictured, full of catharsis or questioning or resentment or something else primal and raw, turned into a numb and relieved slump into our seats, and as much dozing as we could manage. All three of us were exhausted, too much to really register where we were finally going. When we arrived in Seoul, we tottered wearily through Incheon Airport, barely taking in the signage in *hangul*, and Bruce and I turned our carry-ons over to the first cabbie who got to us even though we knew better, paying $200 for a half-hour ride to our hotel.

Jin perked up at the features of our $100-a-night hotel: a personal computer in the room, a jetted tub, and a toilet that came with a remote control commanding the lights in the bathroom as well as blasts of warm air and various jets of water you could spray at your butt with the press of a button. For a while Jin locked himself in the bathroom yelling out things like, "Pulsating spray!" We took a walk, buying food from street vendors: dumplings, giant lollipops of scorched sugar. Then we went, finally, into a real sleep. I want to say I felt something enormous, or Jin did, but that night we felt nothing more deep than relief to be in a real bed.

Seoul is an enormous city, twenty million souls in a relatively small space, high-rise after high-rise (throughout Korea, most people live in high-rise apartments; the very populous country is only the size of Pennsylvania). It is organized into neighborhoods, however, with such a high skyline that as a visitor you rarely glimpse anything of the city as a whole unless you go to one of the truly gigantic towers that loom high enough to give a panoramic view, in which case it looks very much like ten or twelve Manhattans mashed together.

The neighborhood we stayed in, Insadong, teemed with street life. We strolled Insadong for hours every night throughout our stay. We fell in love with dragons' beard candy: spun honey which the chanting young candy makers twirled between their hands till it resembled skeins of silk, then wrapped around a core of nut paste. Along the street young Korean men break-danced, and one night, older women in office clothes climbed onto a makeshift stage to do the Twist. Vendors sold trendy clothes and T-shirts bearing slogans in random English: "Minutemen, Meatpuppets, Angst," read one.

"I love this place," Jin told us, "I'm going to live here." The high-tech aspects of Korea continued to delight my son. The one train we took during our visit had banks of computers and solo karaoke booths, tiny booths businessmen slip into and, presumably, sing their hearts out alone.

We traveled around the country, and when we visited the semitropical island of Jeju, staying in the one fancy hotel of the trip, Jin wondered aloud about getting married there.

"How do you feel about knowing you were born here?" I asked him. "That your birth parents are here somewhere?"

"I don't know," Jin told us, which I believe was no more or less than true. He joked that, when we visited Mount Inwangsan, a mountain outside of Seoul that is sacred to Korean shamans like Jin's birth grandmother, he would run up the mountainside shouting, "Grandma!" In fact, only Bruce climbed Mt. Inwangsan; Jin, a child of the cool Northwest, wilted in the Korean summer heat of ninety-plus degrees, and I had injured my ankle. Neither of us could tolerate the almost vertical climb. Bruce came back raving about the shaman's temple high up on the slope, the eerie sounds of drums, flutes, and chanting, flowers and incense stuck in every crevasse of the rocks.

Before we left for Korea, I had set up a meeting with Mrs. Choi, Jin's foster mother, whom we arranged to meet at Eastern Home, the orphanage where Jin spent the first few weeks of his life. Though I had started the effort probably three months before we left, I only learned that we would be able to meet her a few days before we flew. When we arrived at Eastern Home during our first week in Korea, we were shown around rooms housing far too many babies, all wrapped in pink regardless of gender. The orphanage seemed caring, with a lovely staff, but overwhelmed. I counted twenty-seven cribs per room, more or less, generally with one caretaker, who hopped up and down incessantly locating whichever infant was crying and strapping him or her in an automatic rocking swing. Quiet babies were fed by bottles propped up next to their mouths, without contact, and crying babies seemed to be held only if the automatic swing didn't calm them. The stories I'd heard of Eastern Home from Jin's days there made it sound like a place where infants received more hands-on care, but possibly the visa restrictions have overloaded the system.

One of these babies would once have been mine, or nearly so. I wonder if anyone who worked in the orphanage had loved him particularly, or had thought about his future. I know from my Asian friends that their view of America tends to be the Midwest: flat, enormous, broomed by wind. Though the Korean ideal of geographic beauty is what we have in my funny patch of the US, hidden by a range of volcanoes: mountains and water. I wondered if anyone had imagined this for Jin, before we parents turned up in his life.

The babies lay three to a crib. One, with the wary and pre-scient look of an old man, watched us as we walked back and forth in front of the window to his room. His face seemed too solemn for the lush pink wrapper that folded him in. I have a photo of Jin leaning against the window, smiling, as the baby regards him with what appears to be wonder.

After the tour, we were ushered into a conference room along with our translator, and a woman in her sixties, with short cropped hair and a serious face I would have recognized anywhere, entered. She reached for Jin and held him, sobbing and stroking his face and hair. Jin stared at his shoes, as boys do when they try hard not to cry, willing the tears to retreat behind their eyes.

Mrs. Choi told us stories of Jin's infancy, including some small things and some surprising things we couldn't have guessed: her sister-in-law, nursing a young infant when Jin came along, nursed Jin too. This sister-in-law became very attached to Jin, Mrs. Choi told us, and envied her trip to see him now. Once, as I cuddled the baby Jin to my own chest, lying in bed, he latched ferociously onto a nipple. I always wondered where that instinct came from.

Jin occasionally lifted his face and asked a question. Had he loved to eat? (Yes.) Was he a difficult baby? (Definitely no.) Mrs. Choi asked him to visit her in the town of Taegu, and begged him to learn Korean.

"I was afraid he would think I abandoned him," she told us, crying harder. "I felt so guilty." When Jin left, she said, she had to keep her children home from school for several days; their mourning overwhelmed them all.

Korea, like many Asian countries, has a culture that values gift giving. We brought a small gift for our translator and a series of presents for Mrs. Choi; my contact at the agency said Koreans valued the local, the particular, that which represented *us*. I obsessed about these gifts, driving my family crazy, finally bringing a smoked salmon in a hand-painted Native American box, a bag of roasted hazelnuts from a local farm, and a photo album that began with a tiny Jin playing in Mrs. Choi's home, followed by his growth in our home, our pets, school photos, the garden. I wrote out long captions, hoping someone would translate them for her into Korean.

When we all came together, for our hour-and-a-half visit, Mrs. Choi barely looked at the gifts I laid out in front of her;

she was not indifferent but rather, beside herself, unable to stop crying for more than a few minutes at a time. Throughout our conversation she reached over to Jin, touching his cheek or his hair. I felt guilty, part of a system that, however much it might be justified, creates powerful bonds like these and breaks them: I would never have guessed how intense the grief of a foster mother, who knows she's in it for the short haul, could be. I thought of Jin's birth mother, the reality of whose loss newly stung at me. I also felt powerfully Jin's relief at being in a country, an extended environment, where everyone looked like him.

When Jin arrived in the Northwest as a tiny baby, he came with a bag holding his traditional *hanbok*—a bright-colored, embroidered traditional Korean outfit—and a parcel of photos of his four months with the Choi family; the photos show them delighting in him and spoiling him. The children of the family, preteens and teens, rolled around with him on the floor, spun him, sent him off giggling in a walker. He was always a kinetic baby and I imagine they may have helped create this love of movement, quite different from the sense of inhibition in other adopted babies we knew.

⌒

Jin came back from Korea so much happier than he had been before we left that it felt as if some dark weight had been lifted off of him. He changed his Facebook status so that it read "Hometown: Seoul, South Korea." Kids love changing the narratives of themselves on Facebook, but this change seemed like more than the impulse of a moment: Jin felt for the first time what it meant to come from Seoul because he'd walked through Seoul, night after night, eating food from street vendors and watching middle-aged women do the Twist. And because Koreans were unbelievably kind to him, to all of us.

Bruce and I hadn't known what to expect either; most Koreans feel ambivalent to some degree about their country's policy of overseas adoption, though internal adoption there still has not become common. But everywhere we went in Korea, strangers approached and asked us—in some combination of their halting English and the handful of Korean words we understood—if Jin was our adopted son. When we said yes, they hugged him, hugged us, took photos. People thanked us for bringing Jin to Korea, for keeping his name, for the bit of Korean he could speak. I expect there were Koreans who noticed us and did not feel like hugging us, but these people kept their feelings to themselves.

Everywhere we went young girls followed us, giggling behind their hands and trying out—when they heard Jin speak English—their few words of our language: "Hello, hello, hello," they repeated, and when we said "Seattle" in response to their "Where you from?" (we could not get across "Bellingham") they said, "Oh, Seattle, good coffee!" giggling even harder.

This acceptance acted like a tonic for Jin. The feeling he had was more than that he loved the country and wanted to go back; he knew if he ever did go back, the people of Korea would welcome him. And that, even if he never connected with his birth parents, he had Mrs. Choi and other friends we had made through the church there waiting for him. When we told the Koreans we became friendly with about where we lived, they loved the sound of the alpine mountains and the water. There are landscapes and landscapes in this world, and moms and moms, foster, adoptive, biological, and we learned—and Jin learned—how strangely and beautifully they can all connect.

◦———

To this day, when people ask Jin—as our friend Bobby just did, on a visit we made to New York City—how it felt to see Korea, he thinks for a few seconds and says, "Strange." To follow-up questions such as, "Strange to think you were born there, you mean?" or the like, he just repeats, "Strange. That's all I can really think of to say." He says this, as he said it to Bobby, carefully, as if he's worried about my and Bruce's feelings if he elaborates any further. Strange to think he might have lived in that world, of tiny apartments and vivid streets, rather than this one? Strange to be in a country where almost everyone looks like you, rather than mostly being some shade of Caucasian? Where the two people live who are indistinct constants in your thoughts, who look like you, whose DNA you wear? All of the above and more, I guess. Perhaps Jin's not sparing our feelings but describing that kind of existential strangeness that evades language so completely, a *why-things-are*, like his early questions about why the sun is the sun.

Part V

MY ADOPTIVE
FAMILY

14.

Ages Thirteen and Fourteen:
Old Souls and Young Fools

F OR A LITTLE while after the three of us visited Korea, we
stayed height-wise as three of a kind. Just for a little while:
within six more months, Jin had outgrown us both by several
inches. He loomed over his father and me, stretched thin. He
also began to look startlingly older, even from one day to the
next. Hair fuzzed his upper lip and his eyebrows filled in, becoming the typical marked, shapely Korean men's brows.

As Jin's face and body began to assume their adult dimen-
sions, his brain—improbable as it seemed in this stretched,
grown-looking package—rushed the other way. Jin, from the
wise old soul he'd been as a baby, metamorphosed into a young
fool.

Accompany a friend who was shoplifting? Why not? The
friend, pocketing electronic gadgets, got caught and the store
manager delivered both boys to the police. The police phoned
our house, and that first moment of "This is Officer So-and-So
calling about your son" had Bruce in a state close to shock. He

ran to get me, both of us frantic at the thought of our son in the hands of the cops.

Luckily for all of us, the police report spelled out that Jin had not himself stolen anything. Jin got cited for staying where he knew a crime was being committed and refusing to go when the cops arrested his friend and told Jin to leave (Jin, it turned out, had been terrified for his friend, who upon being arrested pulled out a switchblade and threatened to stab himself). Jin had to write a letter of apology to the store. He also had to go to the courthouse, a visit that scared him to the point where he squeezed my hand in the car on the way over, making my deepest bones hurt, to be lectured by a woman who works with juveniles, a kind but steely woman who explained what being an accessory to a crime meant.

Six months after the shoplifting incident, Jin snuck down to the kitchen in the middle of the night with three friends during a group sleepover, and between the four boys, they swilled down half a bottle of Triple Sec, replacing it with water. I discovered the theft of my Triple Sec, a sugary liqueur I keep on a kitchen shelf for cooking, through some weird maternal instinct that nudged me to taste the bottle. Confronted, Jin sounded like he'd gotten so sick from drinking it that he'd learned his lesson. I didn't punish him.

Over the course of Jin's thirteenth year, he came to hate his small Montessori middle school. He claimed the teachers picked on him and the other boys and he wanted to transfer into a public school, and he resented us for not sending him there in the first place. We considered transferring him out of the school, as he wanted it so badly, but worried about him moving in the middle of the school year, and in a very disrupted year in the public schools. The previous summer, the middle school Jin would have attended burned to the ground, and the kids had been farmed out to various schools in the area. We also assumed that Jin's stories were exaggerated, though as it turned out, many boys had the same problems and ended up leaving. Jin was so unhappy he blasted out of the school one day in a fury, threatening to walk the seven miles home.

If he wasn't seeking out Triple Sec, or reminding us of our various failings as parents, my tall and careless teenager disappeared into his room. He seemed to feel quite certain, most of the time, that he didn't need Bruce and me at all, and tended to respond to obvious questions—"Do you have any homework? Where are you going?"—with a thoughtless but heartfelt "Why do you care?" The response seemed to come less from a desire to give us a flip-off answer than a certainty deep in Jin that he had finished the job of growing up, that his still dwelling with us was some sort of strange, anachronistic carryover from a childhood that felt decidedly *over*.

I could remember that feeling from my own adolescence, though my circumstances were very different from Jin's. Remembering the feeling did not give me a clue as to how to speak to it, though. What can you say? *You are not as old as you think you are,* or *You don't know how life can grind you down if you don't have the skills to meet it*, or even *People can be evil in ways you cannot imagine yet*. You become the Cassandra of awful life outcomes, secretly loathing the sound of your voice almost as much as your kid does.

Jin developed the poor judgment of most teenagers, and also the anger: a sudden change in his inner weather that struck out of the blue, could be about almost nothing, and exploded with the same sense of emotional collapse as a toddler's tantrums: he slammed chairs, kicked the walls, went out of reach. The feeling of cataclysm could be so strong I wondered how many more of these outbursts I could bear. That teenage anger hit when Jin got tired, stressed from school, when someone hurt his feelings, when he felt bad about himself, all things endemic to being a teenager. He thought of whatever he could say that would hurt—even popping out with a few "I hate you"s—then, later, felt crushingly sorry.

When my son was little, I thought about adoption all the time. Mostly I thought about it in a good way, watching his rapidly changing face, his obsessions—with dump trucks and lightbulbs and vacuum cleaners and any device with a motherboard—and wondering where he might be like his birth parents, where he took after us, and where he was just himself. As mother to a toddler, particularly the hot and perverse toddler Jin had become in Siena, I thought about adoption with fear: were we not bonded? Did he have some primal wound that made him resist me? As

Jin grew into a teenager, the fact of his adoption came to the surface again. What exactly did he reject, in that pulling away? Was his rejection of me more complete, more shattering, because we shared no DNA? Did he, ultimately, not love me enough, and on top of that, resent me for taking him away from the country of his birth, the one place where he looked like everyone else around him? Did he need therapy, and could that even help?

I write out these thoughts with question marks, though they struck me then less as questions than as thuddings in the chest, the shreds of darkness that crowded in if I woke up in the middle of the night, as I often did, or if I couldn't sleep. Worst of all, it felt to me as if, when Jin got angry at us, somehow he was always talking about adoption underneath it all.

"You're too old to be parents," he would blurt out, or, "Why did you want to be parents?" I heard, "Why you?" Many of my friends became parents around the same fortyish age I was when Jin arrived. My baby finding me old never crossed my mind, yet here was Jin, barking it out whenever we irritated him, as if to say, couldn't you have let someone else, someone younger and cooler than you, have me? I worried that he was thinking of the youth of his birth parents.

When Jin said, as he often did, "You'll never be the kind of person who understands computers," he seemed to be saying, again, "Why did it have to be you?" It is hard to imagine living in a world in which your parents could so easily not be your parents, particularly as a teenager, when little in your life seems like what you would have chosen. All teenagers obsess about who they are in the world, especially in terms of appearance. I wondered how far the distance between us seemed to him now, living in the world of his suddenly-so-present-to-him Asian features, in a household of three in which he doesn't share that legacy with either of the other two. And with his complement of very different, far more visual, talents.

I worried about Jin. I worried about all the ways in which we differed. At the same time, my own fourteen-year-old self came swimming back, instantly real, as an embodiment of that age appeared before me daily, moping, drinking orange juice out of the carton while propping open the refrigerator door with his foot, letting half of it drip on the floor, or just doing whatever: he seemed—still seems—so *young*. His cheeks kept their young softness, and he slouched to hide his height. He still hates to shower and still loves cartoons. At his age I had had sex and used LSD and tried heroin and meth and overdosed on Quaaludes.

My own history no longer felt possible to me, though these facts have always been among the most real and gut-true things I know. Looking at my son, I could—can—scarcely credit them: who does those things at that age? His eyes still have a boy's shine and clarity. His hands are still smooth and puffy like a child's.

I remember looking at my face in the mirror when I was Jin's age and seeing how feral my eyes looked on LSD, the pupil taking over the iris, huge and black. Jin's eyes, even clouded with an "I hate you," look so young still, simply impulsive, simply reactive. I think of those childlike hands cupping pills, or soaking a paper towel with Carbona cleaning fluid to huff it out of a paper bag in the high school bathroom, something I did almost daily then. Impossible. He was—is—a child. What, then, was I?

In the undeniable reality of who I was at that age, I had to face harder questions. How do I really know what Jin is doing when he's at school, or hanging out in our small downtown with his friends after school, or during all those hours in his room? I worry that Jin is too different from me. At the same time, I worry—a fear that can feel like a hard punch to the heart—that he is like me. Either possibility is unbearable. I can't remember a time as a mother when I felt so much that any direction we might go in would steer me away from my son.

⌒

I dropped out of high school, failing, in my sophomore year. Soon my child will have completed more of high school than I did. This fact has its comedy. Several times I have had to go to the high school for conferences with the assistant principal. The first conference was prompted by a minor problem, a noise-sensitive girl who felt that Jin cracked his knuckles and popped his cheeks to bug her. I sat on the yellow plastic chair, waiting with my heart pounding. (Before going I pulled out my little tan bottle of Valium and stared at it for a while: did I need this? I decided no, possibly not the wisest choice.) Jin's assistant principal turned out to have the same V-shaped buzz cut as the assistant principal of my high school, a clenched fist of a man named Mr. Powers. Though this vice principal turned out to be very sensible and very sweet, he still triggered my fight-or-flight response.

"Jin's a ticcy kid," I said that first time. Jin cracks his knuckles and pops his cheeks even when he's alone. "Can't you just move him?" They did.

The second time Jin got into trouble for something more serious. He stole a girl's iPod and got suspended for two days.

"How," I asked my son, "could you do something that stupid?" and the inevitable, "What were you thinking?"

"She's a bitch," he told me. "A mean girl."

Was he making that up to justify himself? Was she picking on him? We grounded him for a month, restricted his computer use, and made an appointment with a counselor.

"I won't go," Jin said.

"Fine," I said. "*I'll* go. I could use it."

⌒

When Jin had just turned fourteen, the three of us visited my parents in New Jersey. At the time, my father preferred us to stay in a motel; having all of us underfoot made him nervous, he said, and one night in our motel room we three got into a fight. However the fight started, it kept ratcheting up. Jin would yell something, we'd yell something back. It was summer and hot and we were all bored and on edge.

"I hate being adopted!" Jin screamed finally. "You don't know how I hate being adopted!" Then "I hate you," he said, and stomped into the motel room's tiny closet, crammed with an ironing board and extra pillows.

"I'm staying in here tonight," Jin hollered through the slammed-shut closet door. Bruce and I heard the thumping flexions of a boy trying to lie down in a space that could barely hold his body when vertical.

"You can't *fit* in there," I said through the door. "Come out."

"No!" We heard more thumping, and the sound of Jin's head banging against the door. The standoff lasted about an hour, at the end of which Jin came out and wordlessly threw himself on his cot.

~

That summer, I flew to New Jersey frequently and phoned daily to talk to my brother about our parents' care. I was living, mentally and emotionally, in two places, as the frenzy of my son's adolescence coincided with my parents' decline. As Jin withdrew from us, declaring himself capable of navigating the world without too much input from parents—mainly his allowance and the putting on of water for Top Ramen—my own parents became in need of more and more help. They hurt themselves, suffered colds, and broke bones; we began navigating a world of hospital stays and home aides and prepared food.

My parents became more my children than my child was— at least, than he was willing to allow himself to be. My brother and I became partners in a seemingly endless series of caretaking milestones: getting my mother into diapers and my father into and then out of a wheelchair, after he fell and broke his ankle in three places; trying to convince my parents to leave their house, a sixties rambler they moved into when I was away at Oberlin, with little flights of stairs leading to each room or grouping of rooms, and concrete steps in the front and back. They refuse. Because my mother has Alzheimer's, my father has to stay attuned to all the things she can't remember, from what he'd put on the stove for dinner to the daily dole of her medications; if left to herself, my mother will overdose on her Celebrex, Fosamax, Synthroid, and the pills that help her digest and help her move. It seems miraculous that my mother's body can even handle the act of swallowing.

My mother is deaf and her hearing aids do little but annoy her. Though her memories have faded, she knows me. She does not know where I live or what I do, and often forgets Bruce and Jin's names.

She still gets on the phone with me once a week. My father brings the phone to her. "Hello!" I scream.

There's almost no decibel level at which she can hear me: she says, "Hello! Hello!" louder and louder and I keep saying "Hello!" back, until she gives up and hands the phone back to my father.

"I am tied to the stake," Shakespeare wrote in *King Lear*, referring to a sport in which bears were tied to a wooden pole and set upon by dogs, "and I must stand the course." I have come to think of this line when I'm overwhelmed by all the people dependent on me.

⌒

It is striking in these relationships, with parents and with child, how our communion has come to mean all that I don't say to them. Jin has once or twice since the closet incident gotten angry enough to say he wishes we hadn't adopted him. I don't ever respond by telling him the simple truth: that in Korea only a minority of all adoptable children are adopted now, due to the failure of their domestic adoption push and the restricted visas, so his alternate future may not be quite what he imagines. I don't say to my parents when they ask me to cook them meals for their freezer—which I do, dozens, whenever I visit, leaving them in little plastic tubs ready to defrost, meat loaves, pot roasts—that I'm not sure what they've done to earn that privilege. I am present for all of them, wordlessly sympathetic, and I let the gesture of my presence be my word.

I do not hold things in because I am virtuous or kind. It would simply be impossible to say any of these things in a way that would have meaning to the hearer. Neither of my parents recalls the past with any clarity. Jin on a normal day appreciates us well enough, and when he's angry he can neither listen nor reason. To tell him the other kinds of lives he might have would be a meanness, a self-serving one that he would recognize as such. "Someday we'll talk a little more about the why of your adoption," I say to Jin. "When you're ready." And Jin is clearly in no rush.

⌒

My mother has a harsh voice, though she's tiny, and a heavy New Jersey accent crossed now and then with Britishisms, thanks to her English mother. She says "cahn't" and "toffs"—meaning the well-to-do—and phrases like "I don't fancy it." She says things now, in her gruff voice laced with the British "ah" vowels, that I could never have imagined hearing her say: "I'd like to wash my backside now, Susanne," or, "Do you have a spare pair of drawers for me?" meaning a diaper.

My mother's toileting needs have formed an odd communion between us now: she will often only tell me what's going on with her body.

"I cahn't go," she'll say, asking for a stool softener from the bathroom cabinet. If we go out, she hands me an extra adult diaper to carry in my purse. I choose a bag to bring that's large and roomy and will grow heavy with her things, like the diaper bag I once hitched automatically to my shoulder when my son was a baby.

⌒

My life has come full circle. I became a mother with choice and intention. I filled out forms, got fingerprinted, had friends write letters of recommendation for me, as if being a mother could be like any other job. I wrote out checks to cover fingerprinting costs and agency fees. I fell in love with my baby. Then, like any parent of a teen needing to separate, I spent a year after my son turned thirteen wondering what thoughtless golem had taken over the body of my sweet child. Every morning I got my son up and off to school. Every evening I made him dinner and dragged him to the table and forced him to say something to me, even if it was just a litany of "whatever"s. Every night I went upstairs to Jin's bedroom to hug him good night, even after he outgrew being read to, and every night after his teenage angst and anger had appeared I continued to do so. I reached over him in the late evening as he sat at his desk, playing an online game, and I hugged a stiff boy who tensed up and held his arms in, giving me nothing back.

"Good night," I said, and pecked him on the head. This ritual came to feel absurd, but I couldn't let go of it. I couldn't accept staying downstairs and calling "good night" up to him, or not bothering to say good night at all. And so each night I thudded up the stairs, often to a loud and aggrieved-sounding "What, Mom?"

After more than a year had passed, Jin reached up one night and threw his arms around my neck and hugged me back, hard. He smiled, as far as I could tell from my crooked position. Then he pretended to pound the top of my head with his fist.

"I'm gonna beat you up, Mom!" he said, jokey, with actual love in there, palpable as the pulsing lights on his computer screen.

Nothing remarkable had happened that day to signal the change in him; it was a school night, I remember. We had had dinner together, as we always did, with flowers on the table, as we always had. I still asked Jin what he wanted for dinner most days, and whenever I went to the store, though "I don't care" had been the answer for some months. We still had Jin do his homework every night. Bruce and I had opted for the "go through the motions" school of parenting; though Jin seemed out of reach for much of that year, we did the same things. I used to say, kidding, to friends that the best advice about parenting a teenager

I'd ever read was "don't give up on him." I realized that evening it wasn't such a joke. And that Jin had never stopped loving us, or his routines, probably far more than we knew.

⸻

It is difficult to say when my mother's memory began going, as hard as it would be to say when Jin went from sometimes-cranky kid to distant teenager. Looking back, I suspect the process started sometime in her seventies, with a growing forgetfulness and strange behavior that went beyond her accustomed eccentricity to a scattered disconnect with reason. One Christmas, she gave me a patterned bath towel and grew upset that I didn't want to frame it and hang it on the wall; another time she gave me a bathroom mat and insisted I lay it out as a living room rug.

When my mother's hearing left her and she experienced memory loss, I could see some sign of what was coming—her helplessness, her vulnerability—and I believed things would be asked of me soon that I would find impossible. There has always been a force field around me where she's concerned; in a staged wedding photo, she kisses the air some two inches from my cheek. Only my brother has been allowed to touch her. I feared her devolving to the condition of her own mother, needing to be washed, dressed, fed.

But caring for my mother has turned out to be humbling. I feed, wash, and wheel her into the doctor's office, the woman she is now, and the mother she was not. I sit next to her on the couch with a tube of hand lotion, gliding it over her hands, gnarled with arthritis. She lets me. She has forgotten she does not like me touching her, and so, paradoxically, she does like it now.

I have adopted my mother. I have adopted her in spite of her ongoing resistance to being my mother, and in spite of a relationship that no one who knows us well—not my cousins, my husband, not even my aunts or uncles— would argue she has earned. While her memory loss helps this process and enables her to sink into simply needing me, it is also a grace I could not have been granted if I had not adopted my son, had not learned what it means to simply accept what I am called upon to do, and to do it, with little idea of what to expect in return.

Has Jin taught me to love, or taught me to love in a way that gives more than it asks? No, it's more complicated than that. Perhaps Jin has given me, since he was first put into my arms, with his sloe eyes and dimples so deep they could hold a dime, and his deep and generous laugh, a shape to what love is.

Jin has taught me what is possible, and while the answer to what is possible with love is not "all things"—that's false and painfully sentimental—it is more than I could have imagined, before him. My son has brought out strengths in me I did not know were there, and would not have believed. This has happened because of what I have given him, but more, because of what he has given me.

As my boy grows, I see my mother slowly vanish before me. Her hunched body becomes smaller and smaller, losing inches and pounds almost as fast as my son gains them.

As Jin gets older, I confide in him more about my past. I don't want us to have secrets. At the end of his freshman year, I told him—in the car, our temple for confiding in each other—that I had dropped out of high school. I told him that I failed a lot of classes in high school, and that I eventually got a GED and went to community college in order to get into a four-year school.

At first, this fact intrigued him. "I don't know why I'm worrying about my grades, then."

"It's not something I want for you," I told Jin about the community college I attended. "You wouldn't like it. Too many required courses and not enough social life."

One day out of nowhere, also while driving home, Jin kept asking me about drugs.

"Have you ever smoked pot?" he asked.

"Yes I did," I told him, adding that back in the 1960s, people like William F. Buckley Jr. and Bob Hope smoked pot.

"Crank?" Jin asked. "I bet you've done crank."

I have—a lot—but he was fourteen and not ready to hear that yet.

"I'm sorry, honey," I said. "I need to change the subject now."

I imagine my refusal to answer spoke loudly enough to Jin; he didn't push it. In fact, he seemed relieved to end the conversation, to keep me in my safe mother-box for a while longer. As time has passed since I told Jin this detail of my life, he has forgotten it over and over again, in a way that seems too targeted to be absentmindedness. We took Jin out to dinner during his sophomore year of high school.

"How was your sophomore year in high school, Mom?" he asked me, idly. I had just asked him how he felt about his.

"I didn't go most of the time and dropped out at the end," I said, after a pause, in which I thought about whether it made sense to remind him of something he seemed to have deliberately forgotten. I decided it did, for the sake of maintaining honesty.

"Oh. Yeah," he said, and reached for a tortilla chip, dropping the subject.

—◦—

My father remembers that I was an awful teenager, and likes to remind me of that fact. "She was terrible, very very tough, your mother," he tells Jin one night in New Jersey, as I set the table. I'm sure he's right, partly no doubt because of my bipolar disorder—teenage moodiness and mood-disordered moodiness on top of that. I was angry for no reason. And I am sure I acted badly because of how they parented me, and how they favored my brother.

But when I think of my parents' failings now, I remember those "I hate you" moments with my son, the night of lying in bed in a small, cheaply furnished room in a motel, my son fiercely holding the closet door shut as his limbs knocked into the walls. Nothing would have been easier than to give up. I used to believe I couldn't understand my father. But now I also understand how hard it is, the feeling that you're casting your love away on someone who is at least for the moment choosing not to return it. Or throwing your arms around the neck of someone who only pulls in his shoulders, seeming almost to will you off.

⚬

Nearly a decade ago, my father called me on Jin's birthday, a Saturday.

"Something's happened," he said, sounding not quite like himself. "I won't tell you. I don't want to spoil Jin's birthday." He pronounces the word "bert-day." He refused to say more.

Of course, this call had precisely the effect of nearly spoiling Jin's bert-day. I worried all weekend, assuming something had happened to my mother. On Monday my father told me the story: his next-door neighbors, a couple named Rich and Sandra, he in his eighties and she somewhat younger, had died that weekend in a murder-suicide. Rich shot Sandra and then himself.

Rich used to bring my mother fish. He fished all summer and brought her bluefish, and when I visited—which even before my mother turned old still led to me cooking—my mother would ask me to prepare it. It's a strong fish and hard to cook well; I made a stew out of it, with tarragon and other pronounced flavors. When Rich killed his wife and turned the pistol on himself, his fish still rode the ice in my mother's freezer, a ruddy, oily flesh.

Rich's wife had fallen and broken her hip. He felt he could not care for her or did not want to, and their children refused to help, or so he said. He claimed he never saw them after his wife became bedridden, though they lived close by and Rich, my father said, had given his son money over the years. My father was interviewed for the newspaper story.

"It was a problem," he said of the deaths, "of caretaking." He said Rich and Sandra didn't have enough help. Or that's how my father reported the interview to me; I never read the article. My father blamed Rich's children. He continued to tell the story this way, though Rich had a boat in southern New Jersey and a paid-off house and other things he could have sold or mortgaged for household help, not to mention the money he presumably no longer gave his son.

◦———

My father has never been able to explain why he wants to stay in his house so badly. My parents are only in touch with a couple of remaining relatives close to them in New Jersey, and don't see them often. Aside from the murder-suicide, my parents experienced a home invasion a few years ago, by two men with fake IDs who pretended to be with the water company. One herded my parents into the basement, ostensibly to check the pipes, while the other ransacked the house. My father figured out it was a robbery but, of course, was terrified to let on that he did.

My mother can never be left alone or she'll forget she needs a walker to walk and she'll fall, and she has to be walked up and down the short flight of stairs that leads to the bathroom. Whoever is around stands in front of her and guides her onto her walker at the top and bottom of the stairs; she has two walkers for this purpose. To navigate the five stairs she clings to the metal railing and puts her foot forward, when she's going down, as tentatively as a turtle might poke its head out of its shell.

Though my parents' current lives seem untenable, they've probably waited far too long to survive a move. And now that I have lived so much more of my own life, I find it harder to judge my parents, for these things, and for the past we've lived together. My mother's early life is a mystery to me, though given what happened to me with my grandfather, down at the shore cottages, it may be a more difficult past than I've imagined. What my mother gave me as a parent may have taken every ounce of anything she had.

And my father. He communicates with everyone through what he calls "clues"—a coffee pot turned to face the sink to let the aide Irina know she should wash it, an unopened roll of paper towels on the kitchen counter to show Sofia she needs to replace the roll. The people in his life perpetually misread his clues and he is perpetually frustrated about it. "I don't know how she could have missed those paper towels," he'll grumble. He can't explain why he doesn't just ask for what he wants, even with people like his home aides, whom he's paying to do what he asks.

Who knows what clues—obvious to him, thought through carefully and perhaps for hours—my father has rehearsed and left for me, to tell me what he needs, that I have overlooked. Perhaps he has given me clues that he really does love me, purely and unconditionally, and I have been misreading him all these years.

When Jin gets mock-annoyed with us, he says some version of, There goes your nursing home. Now you get the lousy nursing home, the one with roaches.

And then I say, with mock outrage, that I plan to stay in my house and build additional stairs so I can fall down and refuse to leave, just to make his life miserable. And Jin responds with plans for forcing us into the terrible nursing home, hiring kidnappers, whatever strikes his fancy. I can't imagine expecting Jin to care for me, but he's fourteen. When I was his age I lived in a way that probably made my survival seem unlikely to my own parents, let alone my evolution into this middle-aged creature who comes to them regularly by plane, bearing Tupperware.

I flew to see my mother after she was released from the hospital for one of her falls, and she sat crumpled on the corner of sofa that her world had shrunk down to, a couch cushion that still circumscribes her days. When I walked in and approached my mother's crimped body, she cried at the sight of me. She had never, prior to this time in her life, developed a vocabulary for telling me she's happy I'm with her.

"Always glad to see you, Susanne," she says each time I come, a slight, thoughtful stress on the "you."

She talked obsessively, for years after it happened, about the fall that broke her hip.

"It just happened. I wasn't doing anything," she said. "I just fell down."

"I know," I'd say, and pat her on the knee.

On my last visit home, my mother told my father she'd like to move to be closer to me. My parents had passed the stage where either of them ever mentioned moving, so it came as a surprise, not to mention the surprise of my mother choosing to be closer to me. I know she has built her identity as much on not loving me as I have built mine on not being loved. Her condition, which I had a hard time pinning down with her doctor to Alzheimer's or dementia or some other specific term for loss, we call her "confusion." She is confused and she has changed the rules.

To recall A. J. Lieberman, the psychiatrist who argued that all parents, not just adoptive ones, have to adopt their children psychologically and emotionally, my mother has finally adopted me. It has taken a great deal of forgetting, and also developing needs so sharp they cut through her older hesitations. I sense she has adopted me in large part through knowing me as I have become a mother; at Christmases in New Jersey, she watches me as I sit on her love seat with Jin, both of us opening gifts, his head resting on my shoulder. Jin will put his arm around me. She watches me with her eyes canted over, a look at once hungry for the intimate moment I live in front of her, and curious, and somehow satisfied.

Jin rarely left my lap when he was little and we were at my parents' house. Being there made him clingy.

"He certainly likes *you*," my mother would say to me, in a voice lit with surprise and something like admiration.

However the change came about, my mother sees me now in a wholly different way. If she could be my mother again, she would be a very different one. I know this, though there is nothing at all maternal she can do anymore. She might at some point in life have put changing our relationship on her life's wish list, but if she had seen what she'd have to sacrifice to be a mother fully—putting out every scrap of love you have inside you, wondering at times if it will ever return—she would not have been willing. I accept this, too.

A few years after the deaths of Rich and Sandra, my father calls and leaves another mysterious message: "We had a little excitement last night." I call him back. The son of the man across the street, who lives with his father, shot six rounds from a rifle at the neighbor's house. The police came and had a scuffle, took the son away.

"Why did he shoot?" I want to know, and my father says, "He has long hair and tattoos, you know, all over, like." The shooting makes the New Jersey newspapers and I look up the story, though there's no more information than what my father told me—less, actually, as the man's long hair and tattoos don't make the paper. I think of my parents' house as the center of a triangle, poised between three points, the industrial power lines on the left of their house, murder-suicide on the right, gunfire in front. It's mystical, as triangles are: Greek. They're caught in some field made by voltage and violence, one that sizzles on the edges but holds them static within.

The important thing is that they are somehow static together, unmoving and unmovable. Once I was caught inside that house with them and they were caught in their strange field with me, though I moved beyond it. I have to understand that they may have been given the child who brought out the worst in them, as parents, the child with whom they couldn't help but fumble, badly, and give up. And I have the grace of being given the child who could make me a mother.

◦⟋

When Jin comes to New Jersey with me, he spends his time teaching his grandfather how to use the iPad that Chris and I bought, a gift to help my father entertain himself while sitting with my mother. I can tell, watching them together, as Jin creates desktop icons and shortcuts, that Jin is using all of his inner restraint not to become irritable at my father's rookie computer errors. Jin can hardly stand to watch me manipulate a computer.

"No, Grandpa," he says patiently, "don't move your mail into the trash if you want to keep it."

"What's the trash? That thing that looks like a garbage can is the trash?"

Jin buys my parents old television shows for Christmas, like *The Andy Griffith Show*, and sits and watches the shows with them.

"It's a classic, Jin," my father says over and over again, and, "do you like it, Jin? Isn't it a classic?"

And Jin keeps answering, "Yes." While my mother says, "What grade are you in, Jin?" over and over and over and he keeps telling her. After the tenth or so repetition he'll start kicking me and winking.

Mostly, when he's in New Jersey, Jin huddles over the laptop he brings with him and listens for moments when he can pop up from his spot on the floor with a "that's what she said" joke, hissed under his breath to me.

"I can't get this all the way in," my father mutters over an envelope, and that dark head rises up, "That's what she said!" aiming the words my way and mouthing, "That was a good one." My father pays little attention to our chatter and never notices. It took me a few years to understand that Jin is not entertaining himself so much as me, and that this, though it may not look like it, is a deep kind of thoughtfulness, as much so as creating desktop icons and laughing politely at Barney Fife.

15.

Age Fourteen: All Roads
Lead to You

M Y MOTHER DEFINED her role as a mother as making food, and for a long time that's what she did: she made spaghetti and Sunday gravy—Italian tomato sauce—though she didn't want to, and tiny lamb chops with mint jelly spooned from a jar, though we didn't want her to, and when she got tired, she opened cans of La Choy chow mein. She cooked her Craig Claiborne *New York Times* recipes and in what we knew of Asian food, she cooked chicken with rinsed canned bean sprouts and a few teaspoons of soy sauce and called it chop suey.

I suppose I am more like my mother than I care to admit. She did pride herself on cooking every night when I was young, and I cook for Jin and for Bruce, whatever they might happen to want. I make my own cheese and bread and sausage. I have long wooden garden beds of vegetables. I keep a shelf in the cupboard just for things Jin likes to eat—an eclectic group of foods heavy on ramen and beef jerky, carbohydrates and protein—and I feel guilty when he can't find something he likes, even though I know that's ridiculous.

I speak to my family through food. My mother spoke to her family, my first family, that way, though her messages were mixed and puzzling. And food served as her book, her reality show featuring dizzying travel: what she could grasp of China existed somewhere between the bean sprouts and the soy sauce; of India, what small but true newness she tasted in the *Times's* chicken curry, barely spiced with the mild curry powder of the day, and served surrounded by bowls of nuts, coconut, and raisins to sprinkle on top.

"This is not a real *Indian* curry," my brother burst out at dinner one night, when we were college age and snotty. It killed her soul.

There was a hunger in my mother, and many women of her time, for what they could taste of the world, in their cookbooks and on their tables. It speaks now from the pages of old recipes, which I have a fondness for collecting and reading, as if I could page through my mother's daydreams: recipes that declare dishes French or Italian or Chinese due to the addition of, respectively, a bit of wine, a pinch of dried oregano, canned water chestnuts. Every dish was tied to a place, and the farther away that place was, the better, though the food rarely transcended Americana, with ground beef, canned soup, ketchup.

When Bruce and I told my mother about putting in our adoption application, she was neither in favor nor opposed, which was exactly the way she felt about any plans we expressed for having children. She loves Jin as much as she could love any grandchild. She loves him more for being a boy and a tiny bit more, I sense, for not sharing her genes. She is far from in love with herself. She is, on the other hand, utterly generous in her excitement over how much I have traveled, and still travel, whether with my family or on my own.

I have been to Korea and China and Italy and Spain and Slovenia and even more countries than that over the past few years, and I send my mother detailed email messages about each place which my father prints out for her. When I visit, I come with photos. It gives us something to talk about, to the extent that we can communicate at all, and my mother always wants to hear about the food in the countries where I travel.

"I ate hundred-year-old eggs," I said, or rather, shouted at my mother, after my first visit to her following my trip to Hong Kong. "Pig intestine dim sum. Rose jelly with medlar petal."

I had decided on that trip that I would eat the most unusual foods I came across.

"And I had chicken feet."

My mother, who can only grasp some dim sense of what I'm saying, through deafness and her cognitive blocks, cocked a brow at me. "You're rugged," she said, as if travel makes me a man. She pronounces this word *rudge-ed*.

Sometimes my mother stares at Jin, as if surprised that this Asian boy has shown up in her living room, something different, like the words in the ruffling pages of her cookbooks.

I have a mother. I am a mother. I am a better mother than my mother was, I say to myself sometimes. I have been fortunate. I have the right doctors, the right husband. The right child.

⌒

My mother baked apple pie after apple pie. My father loved her apple pie and she baked him one at least every other week, with a crust made from lard she curled from a white and green box kept in the door of the refrigerator. My parents had little real intimacy between them and argued a lot, but my mother did indulge my father, with pie, which was delicious. She had that old-timey habit of cutting the apples over the bowl. Occasionally she nicked her finger and blood dripped into the mix.

"It improves the flavor," she'd say when I pointed the drops out, shiny and red as the peel she left spiraled on the counter, and she'd keep on cutting. As far as I know, we did consume her blood occasionally with her baking, and as far as I can guess she served her sweets to us fully aware of the connotations of that little extra in our food. It's the sort of non-joke joke she appreciated. She had a mordant humor, and one entirely self-contained. She did not expect me to find her remark funny, or care if I did, or if any other family member around did either. She made jokes to and for herself, and though she wasn't a woman otherwise interested in grossities, she found ghoulish things the most funny. The hardest I've heard her laugh was over an old *Monty Python* skit where men cast adrift in a rowboat argue over which one of them they should cannibalize first.

I have a joke with Jin, one we make when we talk about his birth mom and I call myself A-Mom for "adoptive mother" and her B-Mom for "birth mother." The A, I add, is for effort. Which isn't really a joke for him but for me; I too have my moments of self-directed humor. I love him painfully, but the what-to-do part of being a mother didn't come without a struggle and still doesn't. If Jin fell asleep on me as a baby, I became like Mohammed with the cat; I would cut off my own sleeve rather than move him. I studied meditations, like the Buddhist loving-kindness prayer, flopping myself down to meditate as soon as the crying or tantrums or whatever became overwhelming. To this day I page through books on parenting teenagers and scroll through websites of parent advice, double-checking my instincts on curfews, when and how to ground your kid, ever the A-Mom.

My mother's rules for living have been pared down to the nub. The woman who once baked apple pies would now, if we let her, eat only sweets, handfuls of chocolate, and cookie after cookie, store-bought kinds, like Lorna Doones and Oreos. She wants only sugar and eats like a greedy child, stuffing in piece after piece of chocolate and eating very little real food. I imagine this eating has to do with the deterioration in her taste buds.

My father brought my mother chocolate in the hospital after she broke her hip. When the doctors saw my mother's dark vomit, they assumed it was blood, probably from internal bleeding. She was on the verge of getting a stomach scope when someone figured out that she'd been eating chocolate when she should have been on a liquid diet. My mother, it would turn out, had lost 12 percent of her already meager body weight in the six months leading up to that fall, and was down to ninety-some-odd pounds.

In her new, pared-down life, things like newspapers piled everywhere don't bother her, but a few new rules have crept in: her cheap tablecloths must be dry-cleaned, so she never wants to change them; she must wear knee-high stockings every day; she fills herself with Saltines right before dinner.

She will still bark at Bruce and me that women cannot be great, that genius in all things is a male prerogative.

"Your daughter's a genius," said my husband once; he's a loyal soul.

She stared at him. "You think so, huh?"

"Women don't want girls, Susanne," she says, at the news of a birth. "They prefer sons."

"What about fathers?"

"They like girls okay. But they want sons to carry on their name."

Rarely did a day go by, when I was a child, when my mother's obsession with males and masculinity didn't light into me in some way. It might be her rhetorical questions, aimed my way— "Why can't women be great chefs?" "Why is there no woman Shakespeare? Hmmm, Susie?"—or it might be her insisting that I wash my brother's clothes and type his school papers for him. The burden of raising a male child so that he did not feel privileged seemed impossible to me, as if the urge to punctuate my days with naming great women chefs and forcing him to type things would be too hard to overcome.

I remember when I thought I would not be able to parent a boy. But I have a son, who, teasing me, calls me "wench" and yells "Get in the kitchen, woman!"—joking, but not quite, because he knows I love to take care of him. *I have a mother. I am a mother. I am a better mother than my mother was a mother.* My parents can never remember that I have carried on the family name— that my surname is not my husband's—though I explained it to them at length before my wedding, at my wedding, and on hundreds of occasions during the thirty years since my wedding. The birthday cards they carefully choose arrive with the wrong name; flowers delivered to the hospital after surgery come with the wrong name and go to the wrong patient; checks they owe me for buying their Christmas presents for them are made out to the wrong name, confusing my bank. It took me a long time to understand that though they live in a world they construct themselves, at the cost of tuning out everything around them, that fact does not make it the world they want, either. It simply is one they cannot imagine how to change.

⤙

The evolution of my relationship with my parents makes me think even more deeply about my son, my young adult who was once my baby. He plans to try and meet the woman who gave birth to him in three years. I feel, in some fundamental way, I have a different mother now. At some point Jin may have a new and different mother, not in the same way that I do, of course—his will be an entirely differently woman—but in a way that causes him, too, to rethink what it means to have a mother.

I have Jin's birth mother's name, and the name of the district where she lived in Seoul at the time he was born, stored away in an iron strongbox of important papers. I copied both down from one of the endless forms placed in front of us during the paperwork process of our adoption. My belief at the time, based on what our caseworker let drop about reunions, was that we were not supposed to have her name or any information about where she lives. I'm not positive I interpreted the caseworker correctly but that was my impression, so rather than ask I kept her name and district privately in my records. I wanted to be able to tell Jin I had done everything I could to get him this information, though at the time, I acted out of an abstract sense of duty.

I also asked my contact at the agency, when arranging for Jin to meet Mrs. Choi, what the steps would be for him to try to meet his birth mother. I have that information stored away too. The adoption agency we used will serve as go-between, as long as he's eighteen; they will locate his birth mother, if they can, and ask her if she wishes to meet him.

I am no longer acting out of any sense of duty. Jin feels a need to know the woman who grew him in her body and delivered him into the world, as he needed me once to extend my hand into the backseat of the car or to dangle a strand of my hair into his crib to soothe him.

If things go as we hope, Jin will meet his birth mother and start a relationship, and so will Bruce and I. In my mind she is part of our family, a part of my son. But I would not try to meet her without his permission. It seems only fair for him to control this part of his life.

Jin tends to talk about his birth mother, not his birth father. I assume the bodily connection with his birth mother feels closer. My contact at our adoption agency told me he knows few happy stories of reunion. He claims that many birth mothers cannot risk meeting their relinquished children, as they haven't told the people in their present lives about those children. I do know many stories of meetings that have worked, enough that I'm cautiously optimistic.

We have a church friend, an adult adoptee from Korea named Brian, who's in his late twenties. He met his birth mother in his early twenties and has a close relationship with her now, and goes to Korea every year to stay with her or with the half siblings he discovered there. In the process of getting to know her, he became fluent in the Korean language. He loves his adoptive parents and sees them just as much as before he connected with his birth family.

I wondered, when I heard Brian's story, how the process of meeting his birth mother and discovering a second family, then returning home to his adoptive parents in the United States, might have caused him to re-see his adoptive parents. It must be powerful, finally seeing in the flesh a parent you resemble physically, seeing how your nose or your eye shape or your hands came from her, as if you saw the sculptor's clay that molded itself into you. And there is the experience of a country, a language, a culture—a place where you bow to say hello, eat with sticks and not tines—that, if not for an enormous roll of the cosmic dice, would have been yours. His adoptive parents must have seemed more removed from him, both racially and culturally.

I wonder if, with his birth mother in his life, Brian had to recommit emotionally to his adoptive parents—if he had to adopt them back, acknowledging that yes indeed, they still were parents, in spite of oceans and continents and faces that must have felt so instantly familiar.

Sometimes I watch Jin take in my thick curly hair and rounded eyes and Latin features with some version of his old baby thought on his face: *You seem like a perfectly fine individual, but who the hell are you?* The teenage version might be more like, *You are a giant pain in my ass and you don't look anything like me and by the way, who the hell are you?*

I imagine that when and if Jin sees one or both of the parents that gave him his genetic material, it will make him feel perhaps more distant from us. The ties Jin has created internally to the cultures Bruce and I bring with us—Southern American, Italian American, West Indian American—will I expect feel even more coincidental, more vague, compared to the ties of DNA, body, and resemblance.

Jin will have to, as we do with those we love throughout our lives, adopt us. He will understand his ties to his ancestors through us, those Southerners and Italians and West Indian rum smugglers, in a far more reflective and sophisticated way. He will discover how choice and intention can be part of being a son. *I am a better mother than my mother was a mother.* I have had the grace of this boy, Jin, and the person I am with him in my life.

What he will make of this grace of me, if he sees it that way—
and what it has made him—I wonder. He has already been a
more generous child to me than I was, in the past, to my parents.

⌒

When we slept in the same room, because Jin was a baby or,
later, when we traveled together, I taught myself to wake up in
the night to listen to Jin breathing. It would come as a slow and
tiny push into the bland atmosphere of the hotel, one I had to
adjust my hearing to catch, an *mmmmm* breath in, a *hmmmmm*
out, so calm and orchestrated. I woke up to savor that moment
of just loving him, where he was so close I could touch him while
he also existed, dreaming, in some distant unknowable place. A
closeness and a distance that will come, again and again and
again.

16.

Age Fifteen: Moving On

J IN IS FIFTEEN. For the first time he had a birthday that wasn't a family event; in the past we've taken an overnight trip or left town for the day to mark birthdays, to get some time with him away from his friends. At fifteen, Jin would have none of that. He wanted friends to sleep over on his birthday and he graciously allowed us to make him a special dinner, teriyaki and the Korean rice dish called bibimbap and white chocolate cake, his favorite.

Jin has a man's face and voice, and still grows taller and taller. He's thin as a sapling, with endless legs. He just got a learner's permit to drive, so the current surreal parent moments consist of seeing those long legs stretching down to a gas pedal and causing my car to lurch forward. We have two cars, a fourteen-year-old Honda we call our new car, and a twenty-eight-year-old Volvo. The Volvo, an enormous and safe station wagon we call the Tank, will be Jin's when he can drive on his own. He practices on both cars, out in the country, where the roads tend to be flat and straight and empty.

My father used to tell me and Bruce that Jin was going to be an awful teenager, that he would break our hearts.

"Get ready," he'd say. "He's going to be really, really awful. Out of control." If he wanted to make the point more strongly, he would add: "Like his mother."

I'm not sure why my father thought that Jin would be like me. His certainty seemed to stem from the fact that Jin used to have tantrums—though all kids have tantrums, my father always seemed shocked by them—and that Jin had a strong will, kept whining even after we said no to things, talked back to us with phrases like "Wow, Mom, just wow." Jin would roll his eyes and grab my waist to keep me in the room if he wanted something. None of this struck me as unusual; many of Jin's friends were much worse, even in dealing with me. I'm not sure if my father had simply forgotten how my brother and I acted when we were young, or if we had somehow been, at least for a while, more mannerly kids.

We spent a week at the beach in New Jersey with my parents when Jin was ten or so, and Jin's coming awfulness became all my father could talk about.

Jin whined for ice cream, or a trip back to the water. My father shook his head over this.

"You're going to have a very, *very* tough time when he's older."

Perhaps it soothed him in some unconscious way to think I would also suffer with a troubled child. I think he looked for proof that children could just be terrible, regardless of what parents did.

Jin had one tough teenage year and then got over it. He went back to being mostly loving and sweet, hilarious, quirky, in love with movies and good food and the Magic Garden, a kid I'd be crazy for however I met him. I can't quite tell how my father feels about being so wrong about him, so sure I was about to live my own history from the other side.

⌖

Jin has many versions of the affection he first showed me hugging me back while he sat at his computer, the affection you deliver couched in the mechanism of silly aggression, because, as a teenager and as a boy, that's where Jin feels comfortable. It's not that he won't say "I love you"; he will, particularly if I say it first. But if he comes to me he might greet me with an arm thrown loosely around my neck and a "Go to hell, Mom!" He says these things in a stagy, high-pitched voice: "Just go to hell, Mom, I'm sooooo mad at you!" He might jab at the air around my head, delivering it all with pure affection. I've gotten in the habit of swearing right back at him.

"No, *you* go to hell!" and we giggle at our own goofiness.

We brush past each other in the house, flashing the middle finger. At times, when I go out in the front yard to pull out a weed or two, I hear f-bombs hurling down at me, in the same stagy falsetto, from Jin's upstairs window. Even now, writing this, it's hard to describe how clearly this is all love: a pulse of emotion, sent my way, couched in language that somehow makes the feeling acceptable.

One of our cats, our calico Zula, died of cancer during Jin's sophomore year. Like most cancer deaths, hers was long and drawn-out and painful. We finally had to have her put to sleep.

Jin talked to me in the car the next day, consoling me.

"You know, Mom," he said after urging me not to feel too bad, "I don't think you cry that much anymore."

This surprised me. "Why?"

"You just didn't cry over this like you used to. I think that's because of me," he said.

"Because I have you, so I don't cry?"

"No, because I used to be such a little dick," he said, with a tone between a little guilty and a little smug. "I got you out of the habit."

I burst out laughing and mentally recorded every word to tell Bruce.

"No, I think you missed most of my crying over Zula because you were in school," I told him. "But I'm glad you realize you were a little dick last year."

❧

I remember how my brother-in-law David and my niece Laura, when Laura was a teenager, used to play a game of secretly flipping each other off. They competed to see who could do it most creatively. I found their interaction strange at the time, but now I get it: adolescence is an age when you feel as if every move you make is not just visible to the world but broadcast—you're self-conscious, not yet aware of how truly others are not paying attention to you—and feelings that run high must be given in words and gestures that don't break your code of cool. It's hard to get the attention of your parents by running smack into them, as toddlers do, but you still need that attention. So you learn to get it in other ways.

Boys are like this with one another: "Dude, you're an *asshole*," echoes down from Jin's room when his friends are over, with laughter.

For Mother's Day this year Jin made me a homemade card. It's gone into the drawer of homemade Mother's Day cards, the old ones often crafted at elementary school. One teacher had Jin, at eight or so, list reasons he loved me: "becuz your nice" and "becuz you make axcepshuns," he crayoned, which meant I sometimes made exceptions to my usual rules.

This year's card has hand-drawn balloons on the front, and a red cutout heart, along with "Happy Mother's Day, You're awesome it's true," and opens on the words "So for Mother's Day here's a big..." Under the heart-shaped flap I found a pen-and-ink middle finger. It's my favorite card of all.

I tried to get Jin to come with me and Bruce this year to watch Bellingham's June Naked Bike Ride, a tradition in many coastal western cities.

"Uh, Mom? Looking at a bunch of naked people with you? *Awkward*," Jin replied.

"But when I went last year most of the guys wore cock socks," I said.

"Ohmigod, Mom," Jin shrieked. "Don't you ever say those two words together again. Ever. No no no no no."

For Father's Day Jin posted a photo of Bruce and himself on

Facebook, with the status line "Happy Father's Day you glorious bastard."

Why glorious bastard? Jin's thinking of the Quentin Tarantino movie *Inglorious Basterds*—what the connection is, I don't know—but more to the point, "bastard" seasons "glorious" with a little adolescent salt. He mail-ordered Bruce ghost-chili chewing gum as a gift, knowing how Bruce loves the heat.

If my father saw my family at home, with our cusswords and flashing digits and cock-sock conversations, he might still be inclined to think Jin was out of control. My father would, of course, be correct on his own terms—he finds cursing children disrespectful and challenging of parental authority—but all wrong on ours.

Tolstoy said that happy families are all happy in the same way. This has not been my experience. I know happy families that hike and camp together. I know happy families where children call their parents "Sir" and "Ma'am" and even happy families in which happiness consists of video-gaming together. Different as they are, they're happy. We love to go to movies and we love food; we come together every evening at dinner—not just in the act of eating together, but before that, in thinking about what to eat and talking about it and planning it. I ask Jin and Bruce what they want for dinner at breakfast time, and dream up things just for them, like Jin's Dorito Dust fried chicken, an innovation that came from Jin telling me the dust left in a Dorito bag was his favorite thing in the world.

We travel together, planning our meals in advance, restaurant guides in hand, like the Joint Chiefs discussing air strikes.

"Here's a restaurant that makes the best soup dumplings in British Columbia," I'll shout from the computer, scanning reviews, and next thing you know Bruce has MapQuested it and we're in the car, and then sitting in a din of Shanghainese, slurping dumplings.

"Mmmmmm, Mom, can you make these?" Jin says, cradling an entire dumpling in his mouth, so he can bite down and release the lush broth all at once.

"If I can, I will," I tell him, and I always try, though I will never perfect the Shanghai soup dumpling.

Jin dug forty bulbs into the garden with me this year, including the voodoo lily, actually a warped corm that resulted in a four-foot-tall *Little Shop of Horrors* flower, an eight-inch purple-black sword-like shaft emerging from a huge ruffled leaf the color of a 1940s actress's crimson lipstick. The Latin name for this plant is the common little dragon (*dracunculas vulgaris*) and it's pollinated by flies, drawing them in with its reek of decay. We posted photos of the voodoo lily unfurling on Facebook and had a party when it finally bloomed.

This is our way of being happy.

⌁

Sometimes Jin will spend a week holed up in his room, not emerging except to eat. When he's in this hunker-down mode, he eats as fast as possible, spearing everything onto his fork in enormous bites, sometimes trying to get away with eating standing up: then he trots his plate to the kitchen. Jin might spend a week hanging out with Jonny, or asking to practice his driving. He'll bring his computer down to the living room to Skype his friends in the midst of our dailiness. Why he wants to be near us I have no idea, any more than why at other times he wants to be alone in his room.

Jin gets angry from time to time over something specific, like not wanting to sit down at the dinner table and eat at a normal pace, but that quick and molten anger has dissipated, and what for now has taken its place is a teenage air of superiority along with Jin's joshy, insult-laden love. We are foolish, in Jin's eyes, and limited, but lovable in some way. We endured six months of Jin saying almost nothing but a sullen "Cool story, bro" almost every time we spoke to him, a dismissal we heard him give his friends and his friends give one another, meaning, "Who cares what you think?" Now Jin's catchphrase for us is "Don't even try," if we mention a popular movie or hum a popular song, if I play Eminem while riding my exercise bike in the basement, or if we refer to anything at all remotely current. "Don't even try" is much friendlier than "Cool story, bro." It's a reminder to keep to our place, but it assumes we have a place.

I have no idea what's coming in the years ahead or even in one week, one day ahead. Jin's doing well in school and planning to film a zombie apocalypse. He is in the process of building his own computer, a superpowerful desktop he just ordered all the parts for, with a great deal of fussing over the motherboard. I only vaguely know what a motherboard is. Is it the computer's version of me? Will it spoil and embarrass him?

That we expected our baby to grow up doesn't diminish at all the wonder of it, because each day it pays us in new-struck coin:

a face we haven't seen before, a touch on the head—something Jin has started doing back to me, ruffling my hair, patting my head, saying something silly like, "Mom, you're a nice little kitty."

Jin maintains our websites and takes out the trash. He mimics everyone. He's always had a startling gift for doing impressions of people, sounding more like my mother these days than my mother does. He hates school and loves school and misses being in school when he's not.

Jin had one date this year. The girl he dated—a stunner named Erin—invited him out, to a girls'-invitation dance. Jin owns nothing but blue jeans and T-shirts and hoodies plus a pair of shorts, so I took him to Value Village, a consignment store, to buy his suit and tie. Given that he's built like a baby giraffe, all the clothes we could find hung off of him—his jacket sleeves skimmed his thumb joint, and his dress pants stayed up only by the intervention of a belt. I assumed with high school freshmen the standards would not be high, but Erin showed up in a short dress with a shiny blue skirt and her hair professionally side-swept. She looked like a movie star dating a young Korean American improbably wearing a zoot suit. Jin and Erin never dated again: he claims they're just friends.

⌒

Life in New Jersey continues to evolve. This year, a hurricane downgraded to a tropical storm-force cyclone and called by the media Superstorm Sandy destroyed our two shore bungalows, eighty-two years after my grandfather built them. The smaller

cottage was raptured away: nothing left on the spot but a founda-
tion bright with glass bits, a sledgehammer, and a jar of pennies
that had stood on a dresser, upright and unspilled. The rest of
that cottage was washed half a mile away to Potter's Creek, where
we used to row our rowboat and crab and which I was convinced,
as a child, was full of what I called "water moppasins"—water
moccasins or cottonmouths, poisonous swimming snakes that
scared me so much I once jumped out of our sinking rowboat
with my feet in a bucket. We found nothing of the furniture that
had been in the cottage but boards here and there in the cattails.

The bigger cottage was knocked off its moorings, canted on
its side, with the windows blasted out and most furniture torn
apart and scattered. The appliances in the kitchen—the stove
and refrigerator—were also swept away.

My brother and I, during a visit to my parents after the storm,
woke up at five o'clock one morning so as not to miss too much
of my parents' day, and drove down to Holly Park. We wanted
to see the wreckage for ourselves, after hearing about it from our
cousins. And we wanted to say goodbye to the place; a cousin
had gotten an engineering report, and we knew that even the
Big Bungalow had sustained too much damage to be rebuilt.

Somehow we had expected, as it was months after Sandy
hit, that some of the mess the storm left would be gone. But the
only marker that showed someone had been to the cottages after
the storm fluttered on the door of the Big Bungalow—a yellow
piece of paper reading "Unsafe to Enter." After a moment we
realized that the Big Bungalow had actually been pushed back
onto the cement blocks my grandfather had built it on in case of

flooding, so the bungalow sagged crudely but was upright. Other than that, Sandy could have occurred the day before: the ground crackled with shattered glass under our feet, and debris from the houses lay everywhere.

In spite of the warning, we forced the door of the Big Bungalow open—it wasn't locked, but warped from the water, and stuck—and walked in. The walls were gone, down to the bare studs, halfway up, marking the level where the water had washed through; above that point, some four feet up from the floor, calendars and photos still hung on the strips of wall. A hole gaped in the middle of the floor, near where our dining table with its oilcloth had been. The floors sagged and held a crust of mud from the bay.

The blue door, which I had thumbed shut against my grandfather, was gone; only a door frame remained.

With only the bare house left, I saw how tiny even what we called the Big Bungalow had been. Living life there, we hadn't noticed. One-third of the beach across the street was gone, reclaimed by the bay, including the baby pool where Jin had once sat and patted the sand into cakes. Jin had swum many times in that bay, me handing him to Bruce over the wooded edge of the beach area so that he wouldn't have to touch down, feel the foot-sucking eelgrass on the bottom of the bay. That lush seaweed floor held crabs that, if you put your foot down in the wrong place, would grasp your toes in their pincers. I was used to it.

The storm had blown through the cottages from the back. Chris and I found some kitchen things buried in mud to the side of the Big Cottage, an arm from a chair. Most of our household stuff, though, had ended up in mud heaps in front of the house that reminded me of archeological middens. The largest was a game midden, a mud pile that held hundreds of jigsaw pieces, soaked and shorn of their pictures, and other bits and pieces of our rainy-day diversions. Chris and I dug around and found dozens of dice, biblical tracts courtesy of my one evangelical cousin, and a few of our old Monopoly pieces. That Monopoly set had belonged to my mother and her siblings before us, and it had wooden hotels and metal game pieces, no plastic. I saw a glint of silver in the mud and scraped off the little train and the top hat. I had lived, as a child, to get to be that little train.

"Remains!" Chris said. "Did you ever play Remains with Mark and me?"

I said no.

"We would leave our stuff, our little army men, out all over the place and they got buried," he said. "When we found something we'd yell, 'Remains!' The other one had to come and look." Chris shrugged. "It's like we're playing Remains."

We snapped picture after picture. In the back of the house, two bushes were hung with bits of rag rug, shreds of plastic grocery bags like Halloween ghosts, shards of wood.

We dug up things to keep. I took dice, the Monopoly tokens, and a few pieces of tableware—butter knives, spoons, and two large forks shaped like pitchforks—with patterns I remember loving as a child. All the metal had become caked with rust. Just across the street from the house I found a bride doll, snuggled up with a discarded condom.

The bride had much of her body broken off and was only a head and a torso with one and a half arms, fashioned of ceramic with an intact, only slightly grimy veil streaming from her crown. She had a Victorian face, with a bolder nose than any contemporary female doll would have, and a pursed, almost perseverant mouth: *I will grit my teeth and think of England*, she seemed to be saying, echoing that old adage about the duty of marital sex. Given the direction of the storm surge, the bride doll probably came from our house, and could have been my mother's, or even some relic my grandmother had brought with her from England. The doll's condom companion was harder to place. No one using the cottages in the past few years was of the age to need one—all of the parents too old, and the children too young.

I thought of Jin as I saw much of my childhood blown out a double set of windows. The Monopoly pieces, the stoic bride curled up on her condom. Had I been able to protect him from the kind of damage that had almost happened to me as a ten-year-old? If someone hurt him, would he tell me? When I wrote as an adult about my grandfather's attempted abuse, my parents became furious and told me I was making it up.

I would never be angry at Jin over a revelation like that. But would he have the trust it would take to tell me? That, though I've told him many times he can tell me anything, I cannot know for sure.

Jin kept asking me, when I got back to Washington, how I felt about seeing the ruins of Holly Park. He was concerned about me after that trip, remarkably kind.

"It was home to me," I finally said, after trying to explain everything: the sailing in thunderstorms, the bunk beds full of cousins. "How would you feel if you saw our house wrecked, no Magic Garden, your stuff buried in mud piles in the yard?"

Jin thought about it. "I can't imagine."

I realized with a start as we talked that the footprint of our own property, in ruins, would look startlingly like that of the shore cottages: the small workspace, with a bed and bathroom, we had built in the back, is the same size as the small bungalow; in fact, my father used to call it that when he stayed there: "I like your little bungalow." Our house is compact, two stories, not that much bigger than the Big Bungalow. It could lurch on its stilt of foundations as the shore house did. Like those cottages, our house and studio perch at the edge of water. Perhaps I have rebuilt my childhood home, filling it only with what I purely love. But that love cannot protect it.

I pictured Jin, in our earthquake–tsunami zone, digging through his own middens one day: scraps of anime, bits of computer, a shard of vase from the dining room. Random keys pulled from a keyboard. The Magic Garden torn up. I know how much he loves our house. Close to college and an adulthood away from us, Jin will come home and face some version of this kind of excavation someday. I hope he finds the pieces he most wants.

On the flight home from that trip to New Jersey, when Chris and I saw what was left of the cottages, I had my New Jersey mementos in my carry-on bag. The inspector took my bag aside for a search and confiscated one of the butter knives, showing me, when I pointed out that it was a butter knife and therefore not a violation of the rules, what he claimed were two faint ser-rations under the load of rust at the tip.

"These things are all I have left of my old house, after Sandy," I said.

"Serration," he said, and that was that. He tossed the knife aside. I imagined it going into a random pile somewhere. Does anyone ever go through those piles, wondering why someone would want to fly a rusted butter knife home? Remains, I wanted to tell that inspector: remains.

⟋⟍

I returned to Bellingham and to summer, to a home that is present and future, and not just a piece of the past. And that, for now, stands and is safe. The blueberries and raspberries and strawberries are formed and ready to color and the odor of the garden in the evening—mint, honeysuckle, roses, valerian, lavender, lemon balm —censes my nightly walks and envelops my bed, which we moved to be just under the window. It's an olfactory swoon. I choose what to eat at night by walking along my vegetable beds, pulling up greens and herbs, deciding what needs to be harvested. If there's too much mint and cilantro it might be something Indian or Mexican. Arugula salad. Kale frizzled in the oven. Salmon are running in Alaska and we can meet the boats down at the harbor and grab a piece, then later sit at the table with a vase full of rash-pink peonies and mottled bishop's weed.

It takes just a few minutes to grab some herbs, go the half mile to get salmon, pinch kale leaves from the stem. I don't spend much time thinking about the many years it took to fill this garden with flowers and fruit and vegetables, the years it took plants like the blueberry bushes to start bearing. Last year we put in a cherry tree and two apples, and now we wait, as none of them have borne yet. Will they grow into themselves and do what they're meant to do, or won't they?

My friend Edi, who also has a teenage boy, says we should love the moments of peace. I have a garden bed by the raspberries that decided to go barren this year. It once bloomed with dahlias, mostly, and gladioli, and lavender, and I shoveled the space out myself, from a patch of weedy scrub, and carted in beautiful rich soil. It thrived for the first three years. And then nothing would come up, and I put flower starts on top of the bulbs that refused to stir in the warm, watered soil. It is never possible to guess what you will lose and what you will not; you can only dig down, and hope. All of us will have our own version of remains.

The fireworks have begun. It's the Fourth of July, which means poppers and small fireworks have been going off on our street since 10 a.m. We three drove out to the reservation, Jin at the wheel part of the way, in order to break the law—mildly—buying Black Mambas, Curtain Calls, and more smoke bombs and poppers and sparklers than we could count. People are gathering; the neighbors are moving the cars off the street before we block it off. I baked a chocolate pie. Five dried-out Christmas trees lie ready for the night's explosion. I just spoke to my father on the phone.

"Where's Jin?" he asked.

"Outside blowing things up," I said, which was literally true.

"That's good," my father said, "fine," which means he's not listening. He hates the whole idea of fireworks.

The Christmas trees catch fire in our Fourth of July finale, or semi-finale. I don't recall that happening before, but this year each one becomes half a tier of popping fireworks and half a tall torrent of flame erupting from the dry wood. The sight is scary but magnificent, and as the trees fall on their sides, mostly spent but still snapping with sparks, Gene and other men of the neighborhood stomp them out. The final finale is five mega-fireworks all wired together. As they go up, the July sky fires into a brilliant lace of overlapping points of light. Dozens of smaller streams of light rocket up into the air.

I am standing directly under these fireworks, city-grade fireworks, close enough that burning fragments land on my shirt and in my hair. The air is thick with sulfur and creosote, like hell and gunpowder, but with transcendence.

I feel as high this year as I ever have in my life, on a couple of glasses of wine and my son and my husband, who has his arms around me as Jin, the tallest of the kids, films the fireworks in between throwing smoke bombs in the general direction of his friends. He will get out of bed tomorrow grouchy as all hell, because that's how he is when he gets out of bed after a long night, but right now he's smiling, laughing, running back and forth across the street, unaware for a few hours of his newly ungainly body.

~

Shortly after the Fourth of July I go to Santa Fe for a week, working for a writer's conference. In the course of the week, by myself in the Sangre de Cristo Mountains, I do some writing of my own. As always, I miss my son. I return again and again to the subject of him, I describe the world, which unfolds before me in umber mountains scabbed with low piñon trees, caramel mesas, and adobe buildings—a world to which God has long ago set a match and left the most beautiful burnscapes anyone could imagine—as if narrating it to him. In the home of my imagination, Jin is in the backseat of my car, throbbing with boredom at my parents' house and making jokes every time my father, as he does over and over, says of a jar lid or a crossword puzzle, "I'm stuck."

I miss Jin, though I'm aware that I miss, in a way, almost the idea of him; he's in an in-his-room phase right now. I don't see much of him, but I hear him. He scrapes his chair, plays video games that go bing-bing-bing, clears his throat. I think about my anxieties for his teenage years: his trying marijuana, as he's admitted to me that he has, its sweetish smoke going heavy into his reactive lungs; girls; and emotions.

One afternoon I get away from the conference and walk through downtown Santa Fe to the Georgia O'Keeffe Museum.

Her home near Ghost Ranch, not far away, encompassed a view of Pedernal, a flat-topped mountain striped with rust-colored rock and snow. O'Keeffe painted Pedernal hundreds of times—she made abstract paintings in which a few wavy lines and some color expressed it, she did sketches and representative paintings detailed with every crag on its flanks. Toward the time of her death, O'Keeffe, a gray-haired woman in bolo ties who had grown sharp-faced and wrinkled as an ancient Greek seer, claimed she owned Pedernal, saying God had told her that if she painted it frequently enough, he would let her have it. I write this quote down for Jin, and in my mind I line it up with the hundreds of pages of books, essays, poems, letters, emails, text messages I have written to Jin and for Jin. I make a note to myself to tell him that God, with those who love utterly, makes such deals.

‿

Jin has made me the mother I am and I have made him the son he is. Adolescence has in many ways taken him farther away, given me a horizon view of him, like many of O'Keeffe's visions of the broad mountain she loved. He is no less mine, as Pedernal was no less hers.

When I pick Jin up at school I approach the long white building on side streets, seeing the occasional pregnant girl filing out the double doors, impossibly young and doing the pregnant duck-walk down the sidewalk; I see knots of kids bent over low, sharing a joint. Occasionally I see a few boys—it's always boys—taken aside by police officers, loaded into their cars. This is Jin's world now. No more do I know what it will mean for Jin to meet his biological mother, as he plans to, and as I hope he does. I expect he could love her very, very much, but the love you feel for a woman you meet as an adult cannot be the same as, or a replacement for, the love you have for a woman who fed you and held you before you could speak. I don't mean that other love would be less: simply different.

I sometimes think it's confusing that we only have one word for the loves we hold for all the people who populate our lives, as if the feeling you have for your lover and life partner, which has to do with their strength, support, and presence, could be remotely like what you feel for your child—a love that grows from their vulnerability and helplessness and the ongoing vision of a life unfolding.

It is a part of any love, to embrace difference. I've learned to love the times when I find Jin strange to me, as I'm sure at times he, and his father for that matter, find me strange. Rainer Maria Rilke wrote, "But only someone who is ready for everything, who excludes nothing, not even the most enigmatical, will live the relation to another as something alive." All children are enigmatical and cry out for us to accept them as the evolving new beings they are, and not to try to understand them in terms of what we know; perhaps, with adopted children, we are called to do that still more.

"For if we think of this existence of the individual as a larger or smaller room," Rilke goes on to say, "it appears evident that most people learn to know only a corner of their room, a place by the window, a strip of floor on which they walk up and down. Thus they have a certain security." I aim to know as much as I humanly can of who my child is, and—more difficult still— understand it from his perspective and not from mine. I fail every day. All of me wants to apply that limited range of what I know, my corner of the room, overstuffed as it is with armchair psychology and assumptions based on myself.

Every day I sit down in the chair in which I work and open files on my computer. New poems; this book; an article for an environmental magazine on the problems of burning coal. I print out drafts. Every now and then I copy a few paragraphs into an email to Jin: the story of my prayers to St. Catherine, the story of the Magic Garden.

"Did you read what I sent you?" I ask him.

"Mmmmmm."

"What did you think?"

"It was good," he says, tentatively, about the story of our time in Siena.

"Do you want to read the whole book, sweetie?"

"No." Jin purses his lips. "It's going to be a lot of compliments, isn't it?"

"I'm not sure I'd put it that way." I pause to consider how to tell him what I'm doing, in the few seconds he'll give me before dashing back upstairs. "It's certainly about how much I love you."

"Compliments make me uncomfortable," he says, and turns away.

When will he read this book? When he needs to, I imagine.

❏

Occasionally someone asks me if it matters that I did not grow my son in my own womb. Sometimes these people are prospective adoptive parents; sometimes they're just curious, or boorish. The answer, of course, is that it's not an answerable question. I can say that my friends who have both adopted and biological children—more families have both, in my network, than just the one—say there's no difference in the amount of love they have for their children. I can add that loving someone more than I love Jin is unimaginable to me, and probably impossible as well. I think about him constantly. I text him three or four times a day, to remind him of school stuff and to say "I love you." I would text him more but he finds my texting annoying as it is. When I'm away I talk to him daily on the phone. When I'm home I pick him up at school every day and chat with him for as long as he's willing to talk to me—at this age, not long—but we also sit down to dinner together, and I keep trying.

Love is not knowable or meant to be known. It has no quantity. Love partakes of Heraclitus's water: the ancient philosopher did not say you cannot step into the same body of water twice, but he did say that it—let's call it a creek, like the silvery Whatcom Creek Jin used to wade in as a toddler—the creek and you, each time, will be both the same and not the same. Each love is its own body of water.

Mille Grazie

If it takes a village to raise a child, it takes what feels like a small city to write about one. In order to tell any story of my motherhood, I first had to learn to be a mother, and I have endless gratitude for the many brilliant mothers in my life who tutored me by example. First come my sisters-in-law—Susan Lee Beasley, Harriette Beasley Drescher, Gay Beasley Madden and Marsae Beasley Stone—who did me the enormous favor of having their children before I had mine and showing me how it's done: with love and patience and steady doses of finding it all too funny. My V. Street posse, of Stephanie, Al, Harriett, and Judy, became mothers along with me and gave my son his first, best friends and me some of my best role models. So many of my friends who are parents and sorta parents—Kate Trueblood, Thor Hansen, Sara Stamey, Ralph Savarese, Steve Kuusisto, Marcie Sims, Jen Whetham, to name a few—have guided and supported me through the tough times over the years. *DocThor's Guide to Care-Free Parenting: What's the Worst That Can Happen?*, the best book of child-rearing advice never written, has saved my life more than once.

Deep thanks to Matt Hawthorne and Emily Brockman Hawthorne, who have borne Jin and me up over the years. Jen and Marcie, my lovely weekend ladies: in my heart you live in Bellingham. *Baci ed abbracci* to my cyber-sorelle: Edi Giunta, Circe Sturm, Margaux Fragoso, Stephanie Romeo, Jennifer Guglielmo, and Renee Manfredi, Thanks on top of thanks to Ralph Savarese and Steve Kuusisto, for the very rare gift of very real friendship.

For this book, Brenda Miller has been an invaluable reader, coach, and friend, as has my husband Bruce Beasley. Carol Guess has been a much-valued cheerleader, bud, and sounding board. Trina Burke, Michael Dean Anthony, Xu Xi, Patricia Jabbeh Wesley, Dawn Prince, and many others shared their wisdom, and sometimes their stories, with me. Thanks to Tiana Kahaukawila for discussing Hawaiian adoption practices with me, and to all of my Korean Adoption Northwest friends, especially Lauren Soliday, Lesley Frank, and Allie Fee. Dozens of conversations with adoptees, adoptive parents, parents, and experts in child development and adoption inform the manuscript: in particular, Dawn Friedman, Deesha Philyaw, Dr. Dennis Saleeby, Dr. Jane Aronson, and Dr. Harold Grotevant. Thank you for your generous gifts of time and thought. I also thank Erica, Sunny, Meryl, Karen, Lynne, and other adoptive mothers for their warm and candid words about their own families.

An endless debt to Mrs. Choi, Jin's foster mother in Korea. How strange that I don't have in all of my records the full name of the woman to whom I owe so much, who knew and fell in love with my son even before I did. My story begins with her, and before that, with Jin's birth parents. All of these are family, and all command more of my love than they can know.

Mille grazie to Jill Grinberg, my agent, who never gives up. *Ancora mille* to Jill Bialosky, my editor at Norton, for seeing the possibilities in this memoir and helping me to realize them, sometimes in spite of myself! Rebecca Schultz at Norton and Katelyn Detweiler and Cheryl Pientka at Grinberg Literary Management have been instrumental in various aspects of manuscript delivery and production; thanks to all of you for your attention and tireless professionalism. Allegra Huston has been an invaluable copy and content editor who has saved me from myself countless times with a faultless eye and ear.

Bruce Beasley, every year we spend together expands my measure of how far love can reach. I could not be a mother if you had not become a father, and before that, a part of me.

And to Jin, this is yours. As with myself as mother, I bring you all that I have, and lay it at the feet of your beautiful becoming.

Notes

1 William D. Mosher and Christine A. Bachrach, "Understanding U.S. Fertility: Continuity and Change in the National Survey of Family Growth," Family Planning Perspectives, 1996.

2 US Department of Health and Human Services, 2007 Survey of Adoptive Parents.

3 Madelyn Freundlich, "Embryo Adoption: Are We Ready for This New Frontier?" Adoption Quarterly 6, no. 2 (2002).

4 Marianne Berry, Richard P. Barth, and Barbara Needell, "Preparation, Support and Satisfaction of Adoptive Families in Agency and Independent Adoptions," Child and Adolescent Social Work Journal 13, no. 2 (1996).

5 E. J. Lieberman, "Adoption and Identity," Adoption Quarterly 2, no. 2 (1998).

6 Cristiane Casar and Robert John Young, "A Case of Adoption in a Wild Group of Black-Fronted Titi Monkeys," Primates 49, no. 2 (2008).

7 Marshall Schechter, "Observations on Adopted Children," Archives of General Psychiatry 3, no. 1 (1960). It's worth noting that all of Schechter's influential observations in this paper were based on sixteen of his own patients.

8 See Suzanne Dixon, The Roman Family (Baltimore: Johns Hopkins University Press, 1992), and Hugh Lindsay, Adoption in the Roman World (Cambridge, UK: Cambridge University Press, 2009).

9 John Boswell, The Kindness of Strangers: The Abandonment of Children from Late Antiquity Through the Renaissance (Chicago: University of Chicago Press, 1998).

10 Cited ibid.

11 Ibid.

12 J. L. Watson, "Agnates and Outsiders: Adoption in a Chinese Lineage," Man 10 (Journal of the Royal Anthropological Society), 1975.

13 US Department of State, Bureau of Consular Affairs, "2011 Annual Report on Intercountry Adoption," November 2011.

14 Madelyn Freundlich and Joy Kim Leiberthal, "Adoptees' Perceptions of International Adoption," Evan B. Donaldson Adoption Institute, June 2000.